Fast, Flirty, and Fun

EASY QUILTS FROM FABULOUS FABRICS

Sarah M. Bisel

Martingale®
& COMPANY

Dedication

To my sweet and spunky family,
who encourages me and prays for me without end.

Fast, Flirty, and Fun:
Easy Quilts from Fabulous Fabrics
© 2010 by Sarah M. Bisel

That Patchwork Place® is an imprint of
Martingale & Company®.

Martingale & Company
20205 144th Ave. NE
Woodinville, WA 98072-8478 USA
www.martingale-pub.com

Printed in China
15 14 13 12 11 10   9 8 7 6 5 4 3 2 1

**Library of Congress Cataloging-in-Publication Data
is available upon request.**

ISBN: 978-1-56477-997-7

Mission Statement

Dedicated to providing quality products
and service to inspire creativity.

Credits

President & CEO: Tom Wierzbicki
Editor in Chief: Mary V. Green
Managing Editor: Tina Cook
Developmental Editor: Karen Costello Soltys
Technical Editor: Ellen Pahl
Copy Editor: Marcy Heffernan
Design Director: Stan Green
Production Manager: Regina Girard
Illustrator: Laurel Strand
Cover & Text Designer: Adrienne Smitke
Photographer: Brent Kane

Acknowledgments

For my mother, Regina Mitchell, who constantly supplies me with *surprise* fabric in the mail so I can make even more quilt designs, without actually having to leave the comfort of my home. For my aunt, Becky Lambert, who inspired me to start quilting in the first place. To the Utah Quilt Guild for giving me so much inspiration, information, and prizes—who can forget the prizes?

For my hubby, Bj, and my sweet kiddos, Madeline, Mitchell, Elizabeth, and Noah. Your support, love, and prayers have meant more than you can know. Thanks for fetching, pressing, holding, tying, taping, pinning, and loving each quilt I show you.

To my amazing mother-in-law, Laura Bisel, who selflessly took time out of her own schedule to care for my sweet children. Her help kept me sane and on target.

To my friends and family, who inspired me with their own great works of art. To my blog readers, who encouraged me to write this book and gave me the gumption to step out of my comfort zone.

And a big thanks to Martingale & Company for giving me this opportunity to share my love of quilting with others.

Contents

Introduction

As a young child, I was surrounded by inspirational architecture, sculpture, music, and paintings. Walking down the halls of my home, I was impressed by the beauty surrounding me. My parents taught me the importance of appreciating the arts, as well as the beauty given to us by our Creator. I always wanted to be part of this amazing creative process.

When I became a young woman, I was drawn to the art of quilting. I was drawn in when I saw the amazing quilts my aunt made. Her quilts were intricate; the wonderful colors played together with perfection, and they were intriguing to me. Upon making my first quilt, I knew there was more to quiltmaking than a pattern and a few pieces of great fabric. I wanted to learn all I could about this art form.

Over the years I immersed myself in any quilt book I could get from my local library (thank you Canton, Michigan, library). I learned about color, value, scale, piecing, appliqué, and design. Armed with this new knowledge, I became an increasingly better quilter. I spent a lot of time playing with fabric and experimenting to find what worked and what didn't. I enjoyed the process of learning and growing; failures were disappointing, but they were overshadowed by the joy of triumph.

The designs and tips in this book are a compilation of my favorite ideas and methods. As I implemented these new ideas, I noticed my quilts began to shine, were completed faster, and had a fresh artistic look. As you read through *Fast, Flirty, and Fun*, I invite you to test the different methods. Look for the kind of quilts you're drawn to. Are they traditional? Modern? Appliqué? Or are they a mix of them all? You will begin to discover your own style and feel inspired to make creations that reflect *your* inner artist.

Inspiration for my quilt designs comes from people, clothing, experiences, nature, and other art forms. "Sweet Silhouette" (page 35) was inspired by a fun dress I saw at church. A scrapbook page inspired "Cocoa Cakewalk" (page 30). "Circle of Friends" (page 63) was inspired by a home-decorating project. I tell you about my inspirations so you can see that the world has infinite ability to energize us. I hope as you read through the instructions you will remember to look for ideas to trigger your own art.

Before you start any project, focus on the first two sections: "Color and Value" on page 8 and "All About Fabric" on page 10. Nothing will do more to make or break a quilt than these artistic qualities. Your construction might be the best ever, but if the colors and values don't work, the quilt will not be impressive. Understanding these aspects of quilting has done the most to improve the visual impact of my quilts.

The designs in this book have a fresh take on traditional roots. Enjoy choosing a project to make as a gift, for art, or for yourself. You will make the quilt your own by picking your own color scheme and your own fabric. Don't be afraid or intimidated. You can do anything—you have an artist inside waiting to express herself through fabric. Now let's get started!

Color and Value

The correct color or hue in your quilt, combined with the correct value of the colors will make your quilt shine. Whether you're a beginning quilter or a seasoned quilter, a better understanding of these principles will greatly enhance your quiltmaking ability.

The first step in making your quilt is deciding what you want the quilt to do. Where should the quilt *pop*? Where should it *blend*? What parts should draw attention? Should it be bright or muted? After answering these questions, it will be very easy to use color and value to produce the results you desire.

Color

Knowing the color wheel better will help you to attain your goals as an artist. Various color combinations accomplish certain tasks. Complementary colors make each other pop. If you have an element in your quilt that you really want to stand out and make a difference, pair that element with its opposite or its complement. However, if you want certain parts of your quilt to blend, then a monochromatic color scheme is best. Let's go over some definitions.

Hue is simply the name of the color.

Monochromatic colors are all values of a single color or hue. The energy here is subtle and peaceful.

Analogous colors are located next to each other on the color wheel. These color combinations blend together well, because they all are related.

Complementary colors are those opposite each other on the color wheel. They bring out the best in each other, appearing brighter when placed next to each other. Examples are red and green, blue and orange, yellow and violet.

Triadic color combinations include any three colors that are equally spaced around the color wheel. Examples are red, blue, and yellow; violet, orange, and green.

A fabulous way to understand color better is to look at the world around you. Nature provides many examples of the different color schemes. Take a walk outside and see if you can name the various color schemes you see. Also, pay attention to the typically "unseen" world around you. Check out that cereal box, a magazine ad, fabric, wall art, etc. They all have a color scheme waiting to be discovered (and maybe even imitated). I invite you to visit Internet sites for information and read books dedicated to the study of color. The study of color will help you see quilts, art, and the world around you in a different light.

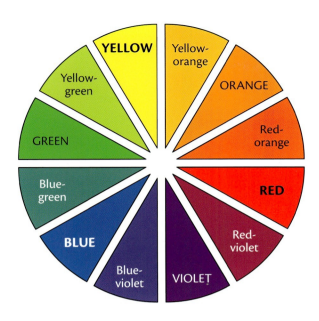

Value

Value refers to the light or dark qualities of color. The illustration below demonstrates the definition of value. A light-value fabric will advance out of the quilt; a dark-value fabric will recede. Many people love to use medium-value fabrics, but I would encourage you to venture into using both light and dark fabrics as well.

Light   Medium   Dark

The value of a particular fabric is very dependent on the surrounding fabric values. If you look at any three blocks next to each other, as in the illustration above, you will find a light, a medium, and a dark value. If the quilt you're making has only light fabrics, then a medium-value fabric will look very dark.

So, how does knowing this make your quilt better? A common mistake quilters make is to use different-colored fabrics of the *same* value. Varying values within your quilt will give the best results. Having different values will make your quilt *dance*, in a way. Your eye will move across the quilt, certain fabrics will be more visible, and some will hide to be discovered later. Enjoy playing with values, and see how amazing your creations can be!

All About Fabric

Selecting fabric is one of my favorite parts of quilting. I love touching the fabric, looking at it up close and from afar, and going through my stacks of previously purchased fabric that have been waiting to be put to good use.

I always use 100%-cotton fabric. I have also learned that buying good-quality fabric makes a huge difference. It not only looks better for a longer time, it's also a pleasure to piece with and to quilt.

Selecting Fabric

After deciding on a color scheme (refer to "Color and Value" on page 8), we get to the fun part of choosing your fabric. For many people, this is an overwhelming process. This is one of my favorite parts, and I've included some guidelines below. Hopefully, these tips will make choosing fabric one of your favorite parts too.

- Start by finding your "star performers," the fabrics you want to shine in your quilt. Choose a few.
- The more fabrics, the better. Consider buying half-yard cuts of 12 to 20 fabrics rather than one or two yards of 5 or 6 fabrics.
- Choose large-scale prints, small-scale prints, polka-dot fabrics, striped fabrics, plaids, and other print variations. Using a variety of patterns will make your quilt much more interesting.
- Some of the quilt projects use Jelly Rolls, Charm Packs, Layer Cakes, or other precut fabric lines. These are great for making your quilt go together faster. However, beware of using fabrics from the same line of fabric; the quilt may not have the value and color differences needed to make it shine. I like to include fabrics from other lines, giving my quilt a little punch of color or value where needed.
- Don't waste your money on low-quality quilting fabrics. You're spending hours and hours piecing and quilting. It would be a shame to see your fabric fade and fall apart because the quality of the fabric is inferior. I began quilting with fabric from big-box stores, and now those quilts are beginning to fade and fall apart; the quilts I made with quality fabric from quilt shops are still holding up quite well. Some of my favorite manufacturers are Moda, Westminster (Free Spirit and Rowan), Benartex, and Windham.

- Forget about matching. Colors don't need to match perfectly, and it's actually better if they don't. Find colors that are close to matching, but are slightly different. If you're using pink, include soft pink, coral pink, hot pink, etc. As long as the colors are all bright or all muted, the colors will look great together.
- Step back. Pick your fabrics, arrange them next to each other, and then step back. You can see so much by doing this. What you once thought was blue looks green, what you thought was a "star performer" doesn't sing next to the other choices.

Ultimately, follow your heart. Always use and buy fabrics *you* love (not what your mom, best friend, sister, or neighbor loves). I can't tell you how many times friends have said to me how surprised they are that the fabrics I chose actually go together. You will know what's best, so trust your instinct. And when your instinct says "no," don't be afraid to put the fabric back in the stack.

Stash building is a great idea. When you're shopping, don't be afraid to buy fabrics that you love but may not necessarily need right then. I have stacks and stacks of fabrics that have no designated purpose; they're just sitting and waiting for the perfect time for me to use them. When I'm buying fabrics for a quilt, I find the "star" fabric and buy a couple of pieces to complement it. Then, I come home and pull pieces from my stash to make up the rest of the quilt. Think of the colors you use most (for me that would be reds, greens, and pinks), and buy fabrics of those colors when you find some you like.

To Wash or Not to Wash?

This is an individual decision. Prewashing your fabric will remove the sizing and excess dye, and it will preshrink the fabric. Quilts using prewashed fabric will have a less puckered and more manicured look. Many quilters today (including me) prefer not to prewash. Quality quilting fabrics currently made are much less likely to bleed colors, meaning you don't *have* to prewash, especially if you're going for a more vintage look.

If you decide to prewash, wash your fabrics in a washing machine with warm water and mild detergent. Dry your fabrics on a medium setting until barely damp, and then press them with a hot iron.

If you decide not to prewash, test dark-hued fabrics (especially red colors) to check for color bleeding. Place a small swatch of fabric in a cup of very hot water with a drop of detergent. Let the fabric sit for a couple of minutes. Remove the swatch and blot it on a white paper towel or piece of muslin. Let the swatch dry. After the swatch is dry, see if there has been any transfer of color throughout this process. If there has, use another fabric. There's nothing worse than ruining a quilt because of bleeding fabric!

The yardage in the materials lists for the projects in this book are based on 42"-wide fabric and assume 40" of usable width after prewashing.

Cutting and Piecing Principles

Once your fabric is chosen, you'll move on to the next fun stage of quilting—the cutting and piecing. Strive for accuracy in both, and your quilt will go together smoothly with successful results.

Cutting

After you've painstakingly chosen your beautiful fabrics and spent a small fortune on them as well, it's a common feeling to be afraid to actually cut and use the fabrics. Don't worry! If you make a mistake,

there are so many ways to fix it. Some of my best quilts have come from making mistakes.

To make cutting precise and a pleasant experience, press fabric well first to remove wrinkles or folds. Cut your fabric on the straight of grain and across the width of fabric unless otherwise instructed.

1. Fold the fabric in half with selvages aligned. Then fold in half again. Make sure your fabric is folded straight and lies flat.

2. Place the folded edges of your fabric on the horizontal lines of your cutting mat. Place your ruler on top of the fabric and put your hand firmly on the ruler, extending your pinky finger off the ruler and onto the fabric to prevent the ruler from slipping. Align a horizontal line on the ruler with the folded edge of the fabric and make a vertical cut. This will give you a clean, perfectly straight edge. Rotate the cutting mat 180° and begin cutting strips and pieces from this straight edge.

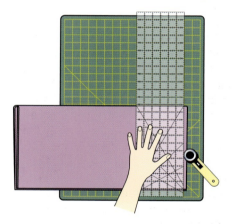

Piecing

This is such a fun and fulfilling part of quilting. Touching the fabric and playing with different ways to put it together make this process an artist's dream. Experimenting with the different placement of blocks brings unexpected and sometimes wonderful results. This is the time to play, enjoy, and break out the chocolate.

Accuracy is the key to successful piecing. To ensure accuracy, pin pieces together. There are times when I feel pinning is necessary, and other times I find it slows me down. If you're new to quilting, try using pins. Also try to piece without using pins to see which way works best for you.

Always use 100%-cotton thread for piecing. Thread pulls on your fabric; polyester thread is stronger than cotton fabric, and it could eventually shred or tear the fabric.

1. Use a ¼" seam allowance and sew with fabric pieces right sides together. A ¼" sewing foot is perfect if you have one. All fabric should be pieced right sides together unless otherwise noted.

2. Before taking your first stitch, bring the bobbin thread to the top by holding the top thread with your left hand. Lower the needle by hand, and as the needle comes back up, pull the spool thread, and the bobbin thread will come to the top. Grab the bobbin thread also, and hold both the spool and bobbin thread together firmly as you begin sewing to prevent the thread from bunching. Let go of the threads after the first three to five stitches.

3. When you come to the end of sewing your piece or chain of pieces, feed a scrap piece of fabric under the needle. Stop sewing when you get to the middle of the scrap piece. Cut the thread to remove the sewn pieces. When you start sewing again, you can easily feed the next patches under the presser foot without having to hold the threads because they're already taken care of within the scrap piece of fabric.

Pre-Wound Bobbins

Pre-wound bobbins are fabulous to use for piecing and quilting because they have three times more thread than self-wound bobbins. Once you start using pre-wound bobbins, you'll be amazed at the time saved by not having to switch and refill bobbins as often.

STRIP PIECING

This method of sewing saves time, energy, and sanity. Multiple strips of fabric are sewn together to create a composite unit, known as a strip set. This strip set can then be cut to make pre-sewn segments or blocks. After strips are sewn together, press seam allowances toward the darker fabrics, or in the direction that makes block construction easiest. After pressing, place the strip set on the cutting mat. Align a rotary-cutting ruler with a seam of the strip set and straighten the edge. Then rotate the strip set and cut as directed for the specific project.

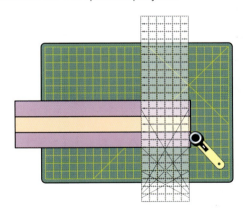

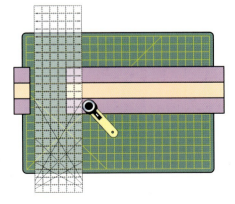

CHAIN PIECING

Chain piecing speeds up the sewing process. After you've sewn the first patches, do not clip the thread or remove the unit. Without lifting the presser foot, slip the next pair up to the presser foot and begin sewing again. There should be a little thread space between each patch sewn. Continue in this way until all your patches are sewn. When you're done, feed a scrap piece of fabric into the sewing machine and sew several more stitches. Stop sewing before you get to the edge of the scrap. Clip and remove the chain of patches. Clip the patches apart and press.

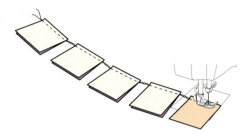

Pressing

After piecing each unit, press the seam allowances. Generally I press seam allowances to one side, toward the darker fabric. Pressing correctly can facilitate construction of the quilt. When the seam allowances of adjoining pairs are pressed in opposite directions, the quilt block is easier to piece and will lie flat. This allows the seam allowances to nest together and helps you achieve accuracy where seams intersect.

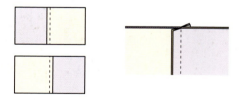

Steam or Not

Why not steam? Steam can distort your fabric and make it easier to stretch. My advice is to keep it dry.

Quilt Top Construction

It's a good idea to square each block before you begin putting the quilt top together. If blocks are distorted, lightly spray them with starch (let the starch sink in for a bit), reshape, and press with a hot iron.

Lay out the blocks as instructed in the specific project. Look at how the color is balanced in the quilt. Move the blocks around until you have found a combination pleasing to *your* eye.

1. To sew blocks into rows, start with the top row and number the first block on the left of *each* row with a number in ascending order. Write the number on a sticky note and pin it to the first block. Next, stack row 1 together, always putting the block on the left on top of the one to the right, continue until all the blocks are stacked. The top block will have the row number pinned to it.
2. Sew the blocks into rows. Press the seam allowances of each row in alternating directions so the seams will lock together when the rows are sewn to each other.
3. Sew the rows together. To make the process easier, join the rows in groups of two or three. Keep joining the rows in this way until there are two halves, and then join the halves to create the quilt top.

Adding Borders

Pieced borders are made by sewing several pieces of fabric or blocks together. This type of border can create a fun, interesting, or more complicated look for your quilt, but can also require a little more attention to detail in order to achieve accuracy.

Typically, borders are cut from a single fabric after measuring your quilt. You may want to consider cutting your border fabric lengthwise, parallel to the selvage edge, since the fabric will not stretch as much along this edge. For larger quilts, this will take more yardage, but the borders will not have to be pieced. In general, side borders are added first, then the top and bottom. However, follow the instructions in each specific project.

1. Measure the length of the quilt through the center, as the edges may have stretched slightly during handling. Use this measurement to cut the side borders, piecing them if necessary.

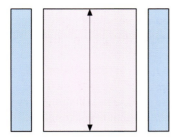

2. Find the center of both the border piece and the quilt top. With right sides together, pin them together at the center and at the corners. Continue to pin the rest of the border in place, easing to fit as needed. Sew the border to the quilt and press the seam allowances toward the borders.

3. Measure the width of the quilt through the center. Cut the top and bottom borders to this length, piecing as necessary. Sew the borders to the quilt and press the seam allowances toward the borders.

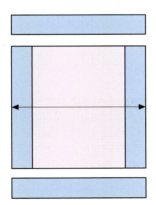

Advice

Quilters are very sharing. As you begin your quilting journey, other quilters will offer many tips and pieces of advice. Try out each tip to see if it works for you. If you decide that you prefer another method for doing something, be confident, and do it your way. Find what works for you, and enjoy it.

Appliqué Basics

Several of the projects in this book feature appliqué. Some new quilters shy away from appliqué, but I use three easy techniques: a foolproof method of machine appliqué, easy and fun raw-edge appliqué, and wool-felt appliqué by hand.

Make appliqué templates using whatever is handy; I often make them from cardstock. You can use plastic template material if you will be using it many times, or freezer paper for just a few uses.

Machine Appliqué

The easy method that I use includes the use of lightweight interfacing. It helps ensure smooth curves and guarantees easy stitching. It may involve a bit more preparation, but the results are fantastic. Take your time and enjoy the journey of preparing the appliqué piece for its big debut. Practice this method and you will soon master it. Here's what you'll need:

- Thread to match your appliqué or monofilament thread (clear for light colors and smoke for darker colors)
- Scissors with fine, sharp points for exact cutting
- Water-soluble fabric glue to baste appliqué pieces in place
- Iron
- Lightweight interfacing
- Open-toe presser foot for better visibility when stitching
- Sewing machine with adjustable tension and ability to do straight and zigzag stitching
- Sewing-machine needles: fine, sharp needles and size 75/11 quilting needles
- Template plastic, cardstock, or freezer paper

1. Trace the appliqué template onto the wrong side of the chosen fabric using a pencil or fabric marker. Cut out the shape, adding a ½" seam allowance.
2. Place the appliqué shape right side down, on top of a piece of lightweight interfacing. Sew on the marked line. Secure the beginning and ending stitches.

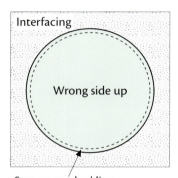

Interfacing

Wrong side up

Sew on marked line.

3. Trim the seam allowances of the interfacing and appliqué piece to ¼".
4. Grab the middle of both the fabric and interfacing to separate them. Then cut a small slit in the middle of the interfacing and pull the fabric through the opening to turn it right side out.
5. Use a hot iron to press the appliqué piece, keeping curved edges smooth and any points sharp.

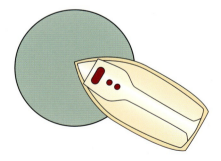

6. Before you begin sewing, arrange all appliqués on the background fabric to determine the desired placement. You should always work from the bottom layer to the top layer. Temporarily secure the appliqué pieces using a water-soluble glue, or by pinning them into place. If you choose to glue, be sure to use small amounts of glue, and then smooth it into place.

7. On practice fabric, adjust the stitch width and length until you achieve a very small zigzag stitch. Adjust and test your tension as well. When using monofilament, I adjust the tension on my machine to 1.

8. Place the prepared appliqué piece under the presser foot so that the needle will go into the background fabric next to the appliqué piece when it's lowered. Lower and raise the needle by hand, pull the bobbin thread up from the background fabric, and hold onto the spool thread and the bobbin thread as you take a few locking stitches.

9. Begin stitching so that the inner zigzag stitch lands two or three threads inside the appliqué piece, and the outer zigzag stitch lands just outside the appliqué piece in the background fabric. Focus on keeping the outer stitches just outside the appliqué to achieve the desired look.

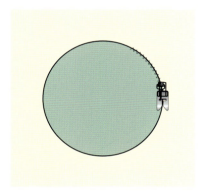

10. Stitch at a slow speed to ensure a smooth and controlled appliqué process. Continue stitching around the perimeter of the appliqué until you're just beyond the starting point. Secure the stitch, and then carefully clip the thread tails.

RAW-EDGE APPLIQUÉ

Welcome to one of my favorite methods of appliqué. I love the look of raw-edge appliqué, and I love how quick and easy it is. It's so simple, and you may find it to be the perfect way to embellish quilts, bags, gifts, and more. Raw-edge appliqué has a ruffled, almost chenille-looking edge when washed; it makes a quilt look rustic and charming and adds texture.

For this method, you won't need interfacing, and you can stitch with a straight stitch or zigzag stitch as desired.

1. Trace the appliqué template on the right side of the chosen fabric using a pencil. Cut out the shape on the drawn line.

2. Arrange the appliqué pieces on the background fabric to determine the desired placement. You should always work from the bottom layer to the top layer. Pin or glue the appliqué pieces in place. When using glue, be sure to use only a small amount, and then smooth out the appliqué pieces.

3. Begin stitching with a straight stitch, ¼" from the edge of the appliqué piece. Make the first stitch, pull the bobbin thread up from the bottom, and hold the spool thread with the bobbin thread as you take two or three locking stitches. You can also stitch with a zigzag stitch if you prefer.

4. Stitch around the piece using a slow stitching speed to ensure smooth stitching. Continue around the appliqué piece until you're just beyond the starting point. Secure the stitches, and then carefully clip the thread tails. For curves, you will need to pivot often, and you may want to use a darning foot if you're comfortable with free-motion stitching.

Wool Appliqué

I absolutely love the feel of felted 100% wool, and I think you'll love it too. Felted-wool appliqué is especially easy, because you don't have to worry about the raw edges. Felted wool and wool felt will not fray, and they can be used interchangeably. Wool felt is a nonwoven fabric made from wool fibers. Felted wool is woven wool that has been washed and dried to shrink and felt the fibers. This hand-appliqué technique is wonderful because you can

HINTS FOR SMOOTH APPLIQUÉ

It's not unusual for large appliqué pieces to bubble or warp if you don't take care to keep everything smooth as you're working. Here are a number of things you can do to prevent this:

- Use fusible web rather than interfacing for your pattern.
- Baste pieces in place by pinning or sewing with a large running stitch.
- Use small dabs of water-soluble glue (fabric adhesive, glue stick, Elmer's Glue, etc.) to tack pieces in place.

take it everywhere you go, it's relaxing, and the final result is so beautiful. Here's what you'll need:

- Embroidery floss in colors to match the wool
- Embroidery needles
- Chalk pencil
- Scissors with fine, sharp points for exact cutting
- Water-soluble fabric glue to baste appliqué pieces in place
- Thimble that fits your middle finger comfortably
- Template plastic, cardstock, or freezer paper

1. Trace the appliqué template onto the right side of the wool felt using a chalk pencil. Cut the shape out directly on the marked line.
2. Place the shapes on the background fabric to determine the desired placement. Either pin or glue the wool felt in place.
3. Cut an 18" to 20" length of embroidery floss in a color that matches the appliqué piece. Separate the floss into three strands. Thread the floss through the eye of the needle and knot the end.
4. Bring the needle up from the wrong side of the background fabric. Use either the whipstitch or the blanket stitch to appliqué around the shape.

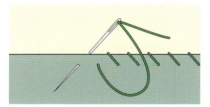

Whipstitch

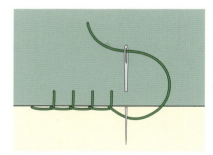

Blanket stitch

5. To finish, insert the needle to the wrong side of the background fabric and secure the stitches with a knot.

Quilting and Finishing

When your quilt top is complete, it's time to move on to the next phases of choosing batting, preparing backing, quilting, and binding. And don't forget to add a label.

Batting

There are many different kinds of batting available. I prefer a thin 100% cotton batting. Cotton batting shrinks slightly with washing and gives quilts a softer, puckered look.

Backing

Using yardage of a single fabric for a backing is very popular. With this option, you can choose a fabric that has a somewhat busy background to hide any potential imperfections in your quilting. If you want to feature your quilting, choose a solid or subtle print.

A pieced backing can be just as interesting as the front of the quilt. I love to use leftover blocks from the quilt top, scraps of fabric from my stash, and other large pieces of fabric. You can put these backings together in many different ways as shown, or use your imagination to come up with others. Some of my favorite quilts have pieced backs.

 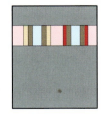

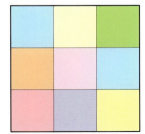 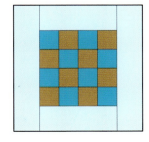

Quilt Labels

I like to add quilt labels before quilting so they'll be well secured. The label can't be removed, and it becomes integral to the quilt. If I remember to do so, I actually piece it as part of the backing. If not, I appliqué it on before quilting. I don't always remember to do this—because I get so excited to finish a quilt—and sometimes I must add it after quilting and binding.

Label all your quilts, including the name of the quilt, who made it (pieced by, quilted by), the year it was made, and the location. If the quilt is made as a gift, I also include a quote or a little message for my loved one. The quilt label can be a leftover block from the quilt or a scrap piece of fabric. Using a permanent marker, print your message on the quilt label, and then press with a hot iron to set the ink.

As an alternative to the permanent marker, I like to print labels from the computer directly onto my fabric. To do this, the fabric needs to be centered on an 8½" x 11" paper, with 2" margins on each side; cut your fabric no larger than 6½" x 9". You can print two quilt labels on the fabric if you want.

First create your label in a word-processing program, and then print it onto a sheet of paper to test the spacing and font size. When the label is ready for printing on fabric, center the fabric over the already-printed page. Tape the fabric in place with clear wrapping tape, covering all edges. Make sure there are no wrinkles in the tape or fabric. Feed the paper back into the printer and print. When finished, set the ink with a hot iron.

To hand sew the label to the quilt, press the raw edges of the label under ¼" and pin them in place. I like to place it in the bottom corner of my quilt so I only have to hand sew two edges, the other edges will be sewn in with the binding.

Marking

I use minimal marking when quilting. You may want to mark lines as a guide, or you may want to mark the whole quilt. Do whatever you're comfortable with. If you're marking a complex design, it's best to mark before layering and basting. You can mark simple designs after basting. When machine quilting, it's easier to get smooth clean lines when the design is simple and you can move the quilt freely. Practice quilting designs on paper beforehand, and the actual quilting process will go more smoothly. Draw a sketch of the quilt, and then use a pencil to practice the quilting pattern on top of the drawing to determine the direction, path, and form of your quilting design. Magically, if you can draw a design on paper, you can quilt it with your machine. Another great no-mark option is to quilt along the print in the fabric. This is a fun and beautiful method, and it ensures there is enough quilting.

Basting

To prepare your quilt for quilting, form a quilt sandwich of backing, batting, and quilt top; then baste the layers together using safety pins for machine quilting or thread for hand quilting.

1. Iron the backing smooth, and place it right side down on a large flat surface (one that can endure scratches and pokes from safety pins). Tape the backing to the flat surface with masking tape, beginning in the middle of one side; then tape the middle of the opposite side. The backing should be taut, but not stretched. Continue with the same method on the other two sides. Continue taping around the backing, keeping it wrinkle free and taut, with approximately 8" between each stretch of tape.
2. Layer the batting over the secured backing. Smooth out any wrinkles.
3. Press the quilt top and center it over the batting and backing right side up. Smooth it out. The batting will hold the quilt top in place as you smooth the entire quit top. Start in the middle of the quilt top and, using basting safety pins, pin approximately every 4". Be aware of your quilting pattern at this point, and try to pin in the areas where you think you won't be quilting. Continue pinning until the quilt is secure.

For hand quilting, use a large needle, such as a darning needle, and white thread to hand baste a 4" grid across the quilt top, beginning in the center of the quilt and working out toward the edges.

Quilting

There are many methods of quilting. Hand quilting is beautiful but time consuming. Machine quilting is much quicker, still beautiful, and something I always do. Whatever method you choose, please ensure the quilt is adequately quilted. The quilt you've made will endure much longer when it's quilted evenly and somewhat densely throughout.

Machine quilting is much easier than you might think. The key is taking the time to practice on scrap quilt sandwiches. The practice time helps you determine the correct thread tension, the best quilt design, and it helps you get in the quilting groove. Never skip the practice step of machine quilting.

When machine quilting, you're free to use whatever thread you like. As you choose, consider the thread strength and try to match the top and bobbin threads in strength. Whenever possible, I use the same type of thread for both the top and bobbin threads; the exception is when I use monofilament thread on top. Don't use monofilament thread in the bobbin, as it will only cause headaches. For a dark quilt, use a darker or smoke monofilament thread; for a lighter quilt, use clear monofilament thread.

For straight-line quilting, use a walking foot to feed the layers through evenly. For free-motion quilting, use a darning foot and lower the feed dogs on your machine. As when piecing, pull the bobbin thread up through the top and hold both the top thread and the bobbin thread to prevent bunches of thread. Here are a few tips to remember as you quilt:

- It's easier to keep an even stitch length if you use the same sewing speed and move in a smooth, even motion.
- Pay attention to the thread tension. Check your top and bottom threads to ensure there's no looping.
- Use quilting gloves. Gloves really help you keep hold of your quilt and move it easily.
- Relax and enjoy. Try not to tense up.

Binding

Selecting the binding for a quilt is like choosing a frame for a picture. It can really add to the quilt, or it can disappear into the background. Both of those options are great, depending on the quilt design. Bindings can be made of one fabric, or have continually changing fabrics. I love to use striped fabrics and plaids for bindings—they help the eye move around the quilt and provide visual interest. Avoid using symmetrical small patterns (like small polka-dot fabrics), as they lose their interest in such a small strip.

Another decision when binding is whether to use bias or straight-grain strips. The only time bias strips are absolutely needed is when the quilt has curved edges. The bias cut (along the 45° angle of your fabric), helps the fabric bend, stretch, and move over the curves with ease. Most of my decisions about whether to use bias or straight-grain strips come from the fabric itself. Do I like the fabric best on a 45° angle, or is straight of grain best? Luckily, many fabric designers are making bias-looking prints, such as diagonal stripes, for those of us who love the look of bias-cut strips with the ease of cutting on the straight of grain.

TRADITIONAL FRENCH-FOLD BINDING

1. Cut the required number of 2½"-wide strips. Join the strips end to end at right angles, sewing diagonally across the corners, until you have one long strip. Trim the seam allowances to ¼" and press them open.

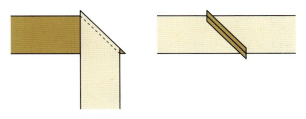

2. Cut one end at a 45° angle, turn it under approximately ½", and press in place. Don't press the lengthwise fold; I fold the binding wrong sides together as I apply it. This eliminates any shifting or puckering, and the binding will lie nice and flat.

3. Fold and place the binding on the quilt top, aligning the raw edges of the quilt top and the raw edges of the binding. Begin sewing in the middle of one side of the quilt, about 4" from the end of the binding strip, using a generous ¼" seam allowance. Stop sewing a generous

¼" from the corner, secure the stitch, clip the threads, and rotate the quilt to sew down the next side.

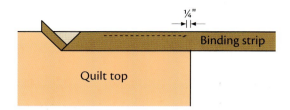

4. Fold the binding upward, creating a diagonal fold, then finger-press in place. Holding the diagonal fold in place with your finger, fold the binding strip down and align it with the edges of the quilt. Start sewing again at the top of the fold, stitching through all the layers. Sew around the quilt using the same method at each corner.

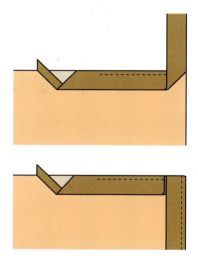

5. When you return to the starting point, cut the ending edge 1" longer than needed; then tuck it inside the sewn binding. Finish sewing, and the raw edges will conveniently be hidden within the binding.

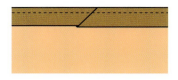

6. Turn the binding over the edge to the back. Using a blind stitch and matching thread, hand stitch the binding to the backing fabric. As you sew, make sure you cover all of the machine stitching with the binding. At each corner, fold the fabric to make a mitered corner and secure by stitching in place.

Quilting Thread

Use quilting thread for hand stitching binding. It's stronger and less likely to fray, tangle, or break.

Hanging Quilts

After making such a beautiful creation, you'll definitely want to display the quilt in your home. To hang the quilt, simply get a curtain rod and the appropriate-sized clip rings and clip the quilt every 5" to 8". This method of quilt hanging is so easy—you'll be decorating with quilts for each season, holiday, and whim of your heart.

Finished Quilt: 18" x 24"
Finished Blocks: 6" x 6" and 3" x 3"

Make this easy and fun quilt to hang whenever there's a birthday in your home. Your family will love this tradition. The wool appliqué is perfect for the layer cake, and once you try working with wool, I predict that you'll be looking for more projects to make with this wonderful fabric.

Birthday Bash

Materials

Yardage is based on 42"-wide fabric.

1 fat quarter *each* of yellow polka-dot fabric, light blue print, and light green striped fabric for center blocks

1 fat quarter of brown print for border blocks

¼ yard *total* of at least 2 different medium blue fabrics for border blocks

¼ yard *total* of at least 2 different medium yellow fabrics for border blocks

¼ yard *total* of at least 2 different medium green fabrics for border blocks

¼ yard *total* or 3 separate pieces of brown wool (6" x 12", 6" x 10", and 6" x 8") for cake and corner appliqués

4" x 14" piece of blue wool for frosting and candle appliqués

3" x 10" piece of pink wool for frosting and corner appliqués

3" x 8" piece of yellow wool for frosting, flame, and corner appliqués

2" x 2" scrap of green wool for corner appliqué

⅓ yard of fabric for binding

¾ yard of fabric for backing

22" x 28" piece of batting

Embroidery floss in colors to match wool fabrics

Freezer paper

Cutting

From the different medium yellow fabrics, cut:
5 squares, 4½" x 4½"

From the different medium green and blue fabrics, cut:
5 squares of each color, 4½" x 4½" (10 total)
2 squares of each color, 3½" x 3½" (4 total)

From the brown print, cut:
5 squares, 4½" x 4½"

From *each* of the yellow polka-dot, light blue print, and light green striped fat quarters, cut:
2 squares, 7½" x 7½" (6 total)

From the binding fabric, cut:
3 strips, 2½" x 42"

Cutting the Appliqués

Trace the appliqué patterns A–J on pages 27–29 onto freezer paper. Cut out the templates exactly on the drawn lines; do not add seam allowances. Using a warm iron without steam, press the freezer-paper templates onto your wool pieces and cut them out without adding a seam allowance.

From the brown wool, cut:
1 *each* of A, B, and C
4 of I

From the blue wool, cut:
1 *each* of D, G, and J

From the pink wool, cut:
1 *each* of E and J

From the yellow wool, cut:
1 *each* of F, H, and J

From the green wool, cut:
1 of J

Organizing the Squares

1. Organize the 4½" squares into the following pairs: 2 brown squares with 2 blue squares, 2 brown squares with 2 green squares, 1 brown square with 1 yellow square.
2. Pair the remaining 4½" squares with each other, mixing up color combinations as much as possible, pairing different blues with different greens or different yellows. Don't pair like colors together.
3. Repeat step 2 to pair up the 7½" squares.
4. Layer each pair of squares with right sides together. Using a pencil, draw a diagonal line from corner to corner on the wrong side of the lighter fabric. Set aside.

Piecing the Center Blocks

1. Starting with the paired 7½" squares, sew ¼" on each side of the drawn line. Cut on the diagonal line, and press the seam allowances toward the darker fabric. Repeat for all of the 7½" pairs.

2. Pair the pieced squares, right sides together and seams aligned. Make sure that you don't have the same fabric facing each other. With a pencil and ruler, draw a diagonal line from corner to corner perpendicular to the current seam line on the wrong side of one square. Sew ¼" from the drawn line on both sides. Cut on the diagonal line, and press the seam allowances toward the darker fabric. Repeat to make six Hourglass blocks.

Make 6.

3. Square up the blocks to 6½", trimming each side 3¼" from the center point.

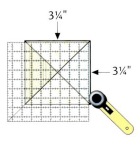

Piecing the Border Blocks

1. Chain piece the pairs of 4½" squares by aligning the edge of your ¼" presser foot with the marked diagonal line. Sew ¼" from the line on one side, and then stitch the next pair without cutting the thread. Continue to do this until you have completed sewing all pairs into one long chain. Cut the connecting threads and restack the squares.
2. Sew ¼" away from the line on the other side, chain piecing until all blocks are sewn. Cut the connecting threads.

3. Cut each block on the marked diagonal line. Press seam allowances toward the darker fabrics. You will have 20 pieced squares, 10 with brown on one side and 10 with two different colors.

Make 10.   Make 10.

4. Pair a brown pieced square right sides together with one of the two-color pieced squares. Place them right sides together with seams butted up against each other. Try to have all different colors, but if that's too tricky, avoid having two of the same color touching when sewn. After pairing, draw a diagonal line as you did in step 2 for the center blocks.

5. Sew ¼" on both sides of the line, and then cut along the marked diagonal line. Press the seam allowances toward the darker fabric. Repeat to make 20 Hourglass blocks.

6. Trim the blocks to 3½" square. To ensure the blocks are squared correctly, trim each side of the block 1¾" from the center of the block. Repeat for all blocks.

Putting It All Together

1. Arrange the larger center blocks in three rows of two blocks each. Sew the blocks into rows. Press the seam allowances in the top and bottom rows to the left and press the seam allowances in the middle row to the right.

2. Sew the rows together and press the seam allowances toward the bottom.

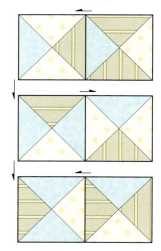

3. Arrange four small Hourglass blocks with a plain 3½" square at each end for each of the top and bottom borders. The brown triangles should all face toward the inside of the quilt. Sew them together and press the seam allowances as shown. Arrange six small Hourglass blocks for each side border as shown. Sew them together and press. If possible, try to arrange the blocks so that no two like colors are touching. If that doesn't work out, make sure that the same fabric isn't side by side.

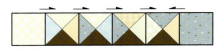

Make 2.

Make 2.

4. Sew the side borders to the quilt center; then sew the top and bottom borders to the quilt center. Press all seam allowances toward the border.

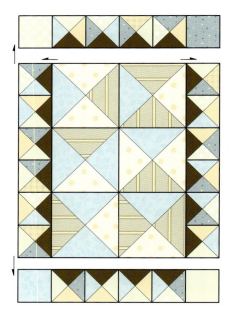

Appliqué

1. Lay the wool pieces on the quilt, referring to the quilt photograph on page 24 for placement guidance. When you have the cake positioned where you want it, remove all but the brown cake layers and pin them in position.

2. Appliqué the brown wool cake layers using three strands of brown embroidery floss to match. Use

a blanket stitch or whip stitch, referring to "Wool Appliqué" on page 17.

3. After you have completed appliquéing the cake, add the frosting, candle, and flame, pinning and then stitching each shape with matching embroidery floss.

Choose Your Colors

Feel free to use a different or contrasting color of embroidery floss. This is your quilt, and you can make it look absolutely amazing!

4. Appliqué the brown wool circles to the corner blocks. Continue with the smaller, different-colored wool circles.

Completing the Quilt

Refer to "Quilting and Finishing," beginning on page 19 for details as needed. I stipple quilted around the cake and the border. I stitched double rows of straight stitching in the brown triangles of the border to create a zigzag pattern.

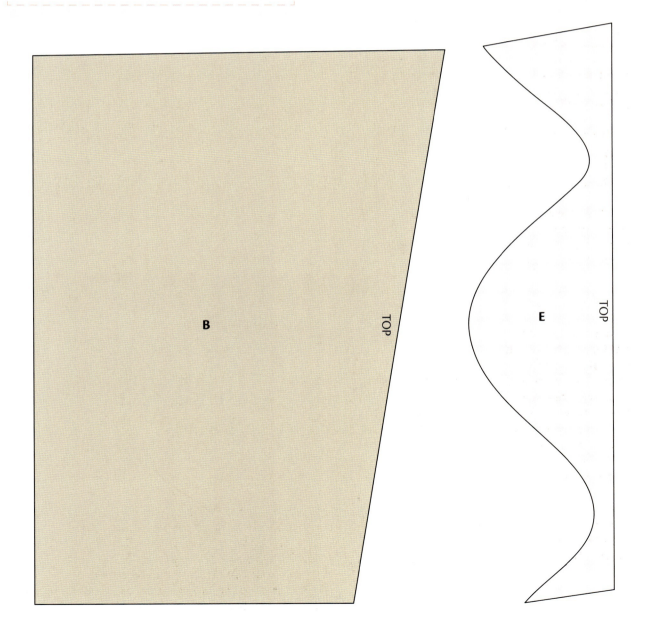

B

TOP

E

TOP

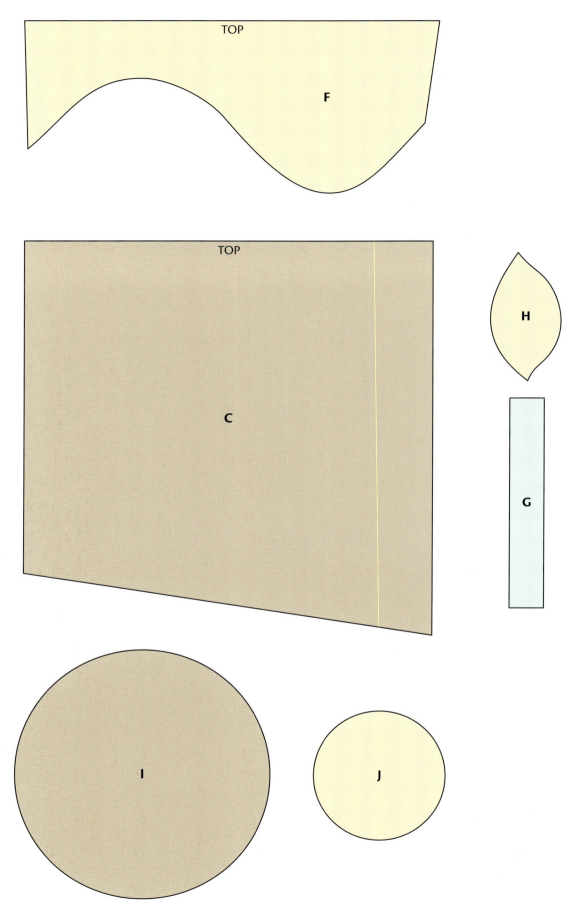

TOP

F

TOP

C

H

G

I

J

TOP

A

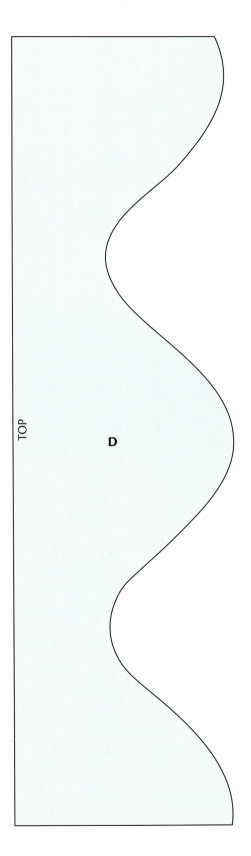

TOP

D

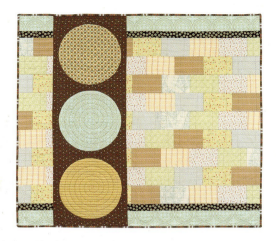

Finished Quilt: 52½" x 48"

Chocolate cake is a favorite in our household. This quilt's inspiration came from the many different ways we like to prepare our favorite dessert—baked in the round and layered, swirled with icing, or as a sheet cake cut into generous rectangular serving pieces. It's amazing what joy a little chocolate and a warm quilt can bring.

Cocoa Cakewalk

Materials

Yardage is based on 42"-wide fabric.

1 fat quarter *each* of 7 different light-value prints
1½ yards of dark print for circle background
3 fat quarters of prints for circle appliqués
⅓ yard of light blue print for outer border
¼ yard of medium dark print for inner border
½ yard of striped fabric for binding
3 yards of fabric for backing
54" x 59" piece of batting
1½ yards of 20"-wide lightweight interfacing

Cutting

From *each* of the 7 different light-value fat quarters, cut:
8 rectangles, 4½" x 6½" (56 total; 2 are extra)

From the medium dark print, cut:
2 strips, 2½" x 42"

From the light blue print, cut:
2 strips, 4½" x 42"

From *each* of the 3 fat quarters of prints for circles, cut:
1 circle*

From the dark print for circle background, cut on the *lengthwise* grain:
1 strip, 17" x 48½"

From the striped fabric, cut:
6 strips, 2½" x 42"

*Create a full-circle template from the quarter-circle pattern on page 34. Using the template, trace a circle on the wrong side of each of the three fat quarters. Cut out the circles, adding a ½" seam allowance all around.

Piecing

1. Arrange the 4½" x 6½" rectangles in nine horizontal rows of six rectangles each. Number the rows 1 through 9, with 1 being the top row. Sew the rectangles into rows, 4½" sides together. Press seam allowances of odd-numbered rows to the left; press even-numbered rows to the right.

   Note: For easier construction, the outer rectangles in the offset rows will be the same fabric. This is not the case in the quilt shown.

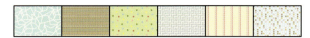

   Make 9.

2. Sew rows 1, 3, 5, 7, and 9 into a loop, first marking the left rectangle of each row with a pin. Press the seam allowances in the same direction as the rest of the row.

   Sew together.

3. Cut the loop rows by cutting the marked block in half (3" from the seam line).

   3"   3"

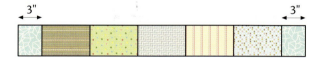

4. Sew the nine rows together. Press seam allowances in one direction.

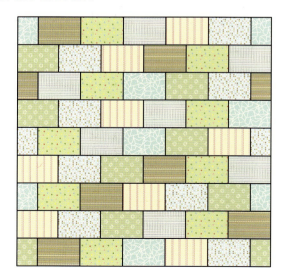

5. Join a medium dark inner-border strip to the light blue outer-border strip. Make two. Press the seam allowances toward the inner border.

   Make 2.

6. Referring to "Adding Borders" on page 14, measure the quilt and add the border units to the top and bottom. Press the seam allowances toward the borders.

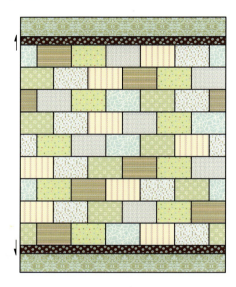

7. Cut the quilt top, 7½" from the left edge.

   7½"

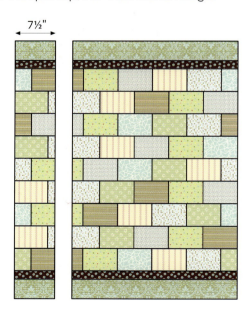

Appliqué

1. Find the center of the circle background strip by folding the strip in half in both directions; finger-press to leave a crease.
2. Follow the instructions in "Machine Appliqué" on page 16 to prepare the circles for appliqué. Fold the center circle in half twice and crease well, so you can see the middle line clearly. Fold the other circles in half once and crease.

3. Starting with the middle circle, pin it to the center of the background strip. Match up the middle crease in your circle with the middle crease of the background strip to ensure that your circle is centered.
4. Pin the remaining circles in the same manner. The circles should be spaced 1½" from each other.
5. Appliqué the circles by machine, referring to "Machine Appliqué" as needed.
6. Join the circle background to the quilt top by sewing it between the smaller side piece and the larger section of the quilt top. Press seam allowances toward the circle strip.

Completing the Quilt

Refer to "Quilting and Finishing," beginning on page 19 for details as needed. I quilted spirals in each of the large circles; the body of the quilt was quilted in a grid pattern, and the borders were quilted by following the print in the fabric.

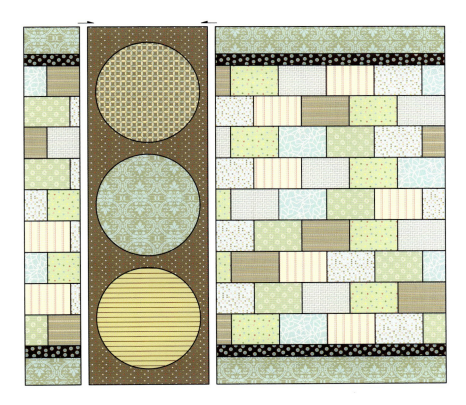

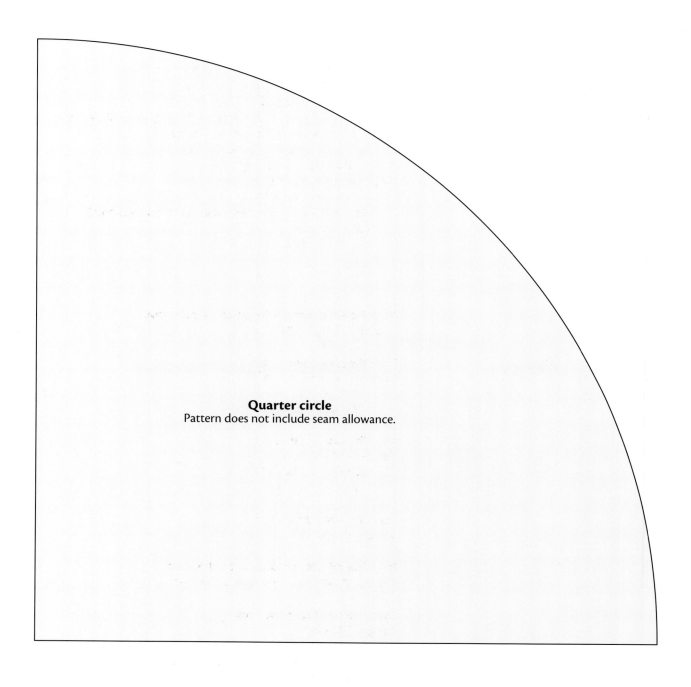

Quarter circle
Pattern does not include seam allowance.

Finished Quilt: 31½" x 31½"

This sweet quilt offers a way to use a fabulous big print in a new and unique way. Choose a favorite fabric, and you'll be able to enjoy it for years. The design is simple and can easily be put together in just one day. Depending on the fabric you choose, this quilt would be perfect for a table topper, a baby quilt, or for something beautiful to adorn a wall.

Sweet Silhouette

Materials

Yardage is based on 42"-wide fabric.

⅞ yard of white print for outer border
¾ yard of print for scalloped border
1 fat quarter of large-scale print (or ⅝ yard) for quilt center
¼ yard of brown print for middle border
⅛ yard of green plaid for inner border
⅜ yard of fabric for binding
1⅛ yards of fabric for backing
36" x 36" piece of batting
2½ yards of 20"-wide lightweight interfacing (optional)
Template material
Water-soluble fabric glue

Cutting

From the fat quarter of large-scale print, cut:
1 square, 17½" x 17½"

From the green plaid, cut:
2 strips, 1" x 42"; cut into:
      2 strips 1" x 17½"
      2 strips, 1" x 18½"

From the brown print, cut:
2 strips, 1¾" x 42"; cut into:
      2 strips, 1¾" x 18½"
      2 strips, 1¾" x 21"

From the white print, cut:
4 strips, 6" x 38"

From the print for scalloped border, cut:
4 strips, 5" x 42" for raw-edge appliqué*

From the binding fabric, cut:
4 strips, 2½" x 42"

For machine appliqué using interfacing, cut:
4 strips, 5½" x 42"

Assembling the Quilt

1. Sew the 1" x 17½" green plaid inner-border strips to two opposite sides of the center square. Press seam allowances toward the inner border. Sew the 18½" strips to the remaining sides of the quilt center. Press the seam allowances toward the inner border.

2. Add the brown print middle-border strips in the same manner as in steps 1 and 2.

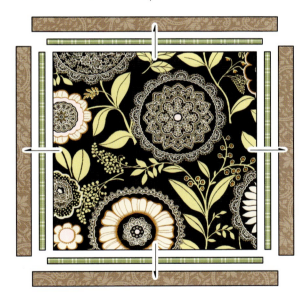

3. The white outer borders have mitered corners. Pin the center of one 6" x 38" border strip to the center of the quilt top, right sides together. Add additional pins and sew the border to the quilt, starting ¼" from the top corner and finishing ¼" from the bottom corner. There will be excess border fabric extending beyond the quilt top.

Press seam allowances toward the border strip. Repeat for the remaining three sides.

4. Lay the quilt out wrong side up, with one of the border strips lying over the other border strip, so the border strips make a 90° angle. Use a large acrylic ruler with a 45° line marked on it. Align the 45° line with the folded edge of the border fabric so that the point of the ruler intersects the 90° angle of the overlapped borders. With a pencil, mark along the ruler's edge from the corner seam to the outer edge.

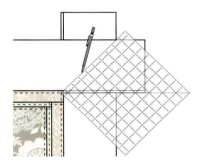

5. Fold the quilt diagonally with right sides together and align the two border pieces. Make sure the quilt and borders are lying flat. Pin the borders together along the marked line.

6. Begin sewing at the inside corner on the marked line. Take a couple stitches, and then backstitch to secure the stitching. Be careful not to sew inside the corner seam line, as this will make it pucker (but should that happen you can always use your handy seam ripper to remove a stitch).

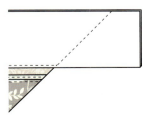

7. Open up the mitered corner. If it lies flat, congratulations, you did it! Trim the seam allowances to ¼" and press them to one side. Repeat at each corner.

Making the Scalloped Border

1. Place two strips for the scalloped border, right sides together, aligning ends and edges. Mark a 45° angle about ½" from the end of the strip. Sew on the marked line. Continue with the other two scalloped-border strips. Trim seam allowances to ¼" and press them to one side. This will create the miters on two corners of the scalloped border.

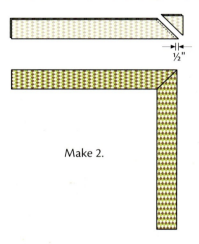

½"

Make 2.

2. To miter the remaining corners, place the finished corners right sides together. Measure 21½" from the inside corner to each end and mark. From each mark, draw a line at a 45° angle, in the opposite direction from the already sewn corners. Sew on the drawn line. Do not trim yet.

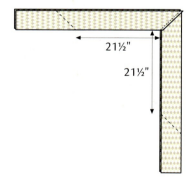

21½"

21½"

3. Place the scalloped border on the quilt top and check to make sure it fits properly. Align the raw edges of the white background border and the scalloped border around the edge of the quilt. Align the mitered seams and corners. When the scalloped border fits correctly, trim the seam allowances of the last mitered corners to ¼" and press the seam allowances to one side.

4. Make scalloped-border templates using the patterns on pages 40 and 41. Mark the scallops on the scalloped-border fabric. Start with the *corner template*, and mark each corner. To mark the remaining scallops, find the center of each side, and align the center of the *side-scallop* template. Mark the center scallop on the fabric, and then mark the two side scallops. If the scallops don't fit exactly, adjust the length of the joining valleys.

5. For raw-edge appliqué, use scissors to cut along the marked line. If using interfacing, add a ½" seam allowance.

6. Using a water-soluble glue, adhere the scalloped border to the quilt top to prepare it for quilting. You can use the raw-edge appliqué method to stitch the scallops on before quilting, or you can appliqué and quilt at the same time, and save yourself a step. Do whatever you're comfortable with.

Completing the Quilt

Refer to "Quilting and Finishing" beginning on page 19 for details as needed. In the center of this quilt, I quilted around the motifs in the print. I quilted a straight line on either side of the small and larger inner borders and a small free-motion scroll in the brown border. The white border was stipple quilted, and the scalloped border was quilted in a scallop pattern following the print of the fabric.

Variations on a Theme

You can easily vary the size of the center fabric to make a much larger quilt using this same general method. If you want to make it more interesting, try using multiple fabrics of the same color in the scalloped border. Have fun and be creative!

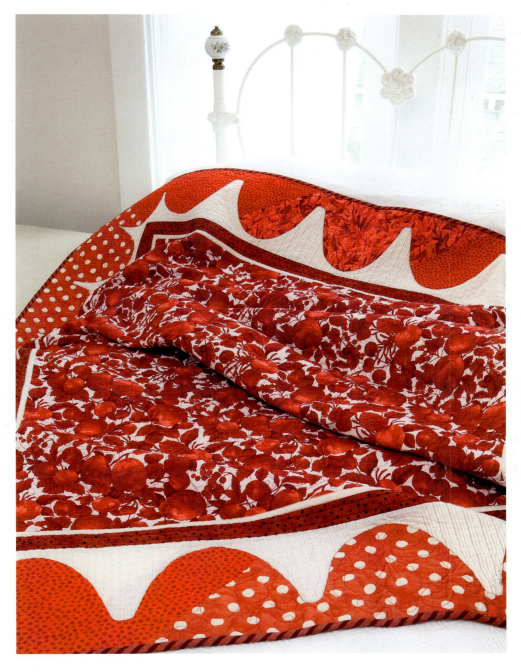

Red Sweet Silhouette, 56" x 70"

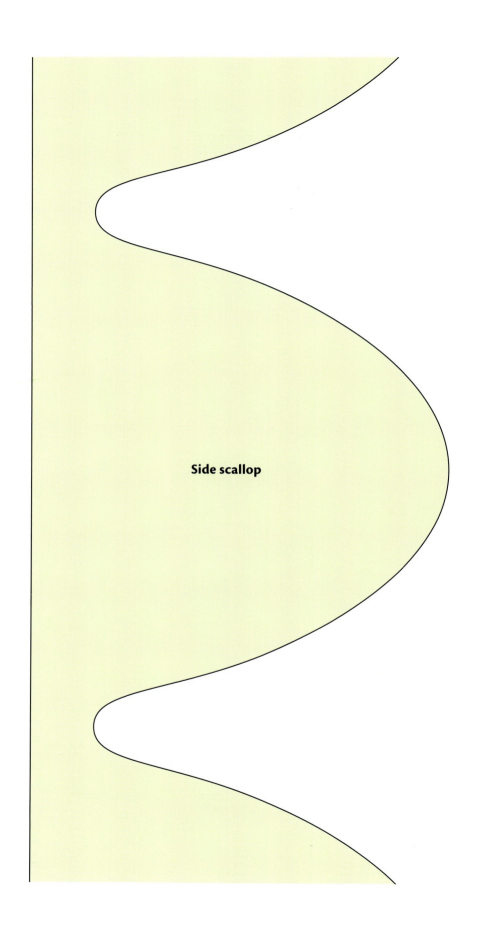

Side scallop

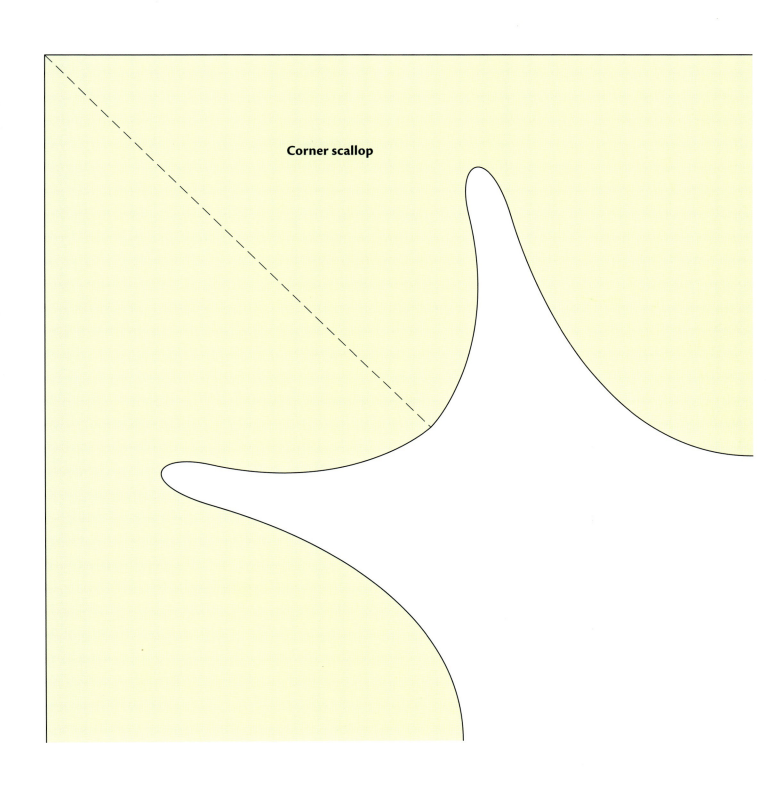

Corner scallop

Finished Quilt: 35½" x 37"

I just love this sock-monkey print. I included it in two different colorways to make this fun, strippy quilt so that I could cherish it for years to come. Include your own preferred prints and use coordinating strips or leftover fabrics to make a quilt featuring an adorable print—one that's too delightful to sit hidden away on your fabric shelf.

Monkey in the Middle

Materials

Yardage is based on 42"-wide fabric.

⅛ yard *each* of 11 different, striped, polka-dot, checked, and plaid fabrics
¾ yard of green diagonally striped fabric for border
⅜ yard of brown fabric for sashing
¼ yard of light blue monkey (or other) print
⅛ yard of light green monkey (or other) print
⅛ yard of light green print for sashing
⅜ yard of diagonally striped fabric for binding
1¼ yards of fabric for backing
40" x 43" piece of batting

Cutting

From the light blue monkey print, cut:
2 strips, 3½" x 22"

From the light green monkey print, cut:
1 strip, 3½" x 22"

From *each of 4* striped, polka-dot, checked, and plaid fabrics, cut:
1 strip, 1½" x 22" strips (4 total)

From *each of 3* striped, polka-dot, checked, and plaid fabrics, cut:
1 strip, 2½" x 22" (3 total)

From *each of 4* striped, polka-dot, checked, and plaid fabrics, cut:
1 strip, 2" x 22" (4 total)

From the brown fabric, cut:
4 strips, 1¼" x 25½"
2 strips, 1½" x 25½"
2 strips, 1½" x 26"

From the light green print, cut:
2 strips, 1" x 25½"

From the green diagonally striped fabric, cut:
4 strips, 5½" x 42"; cut into:
    2 strips, 5½" x 26"
    2 strips, 5½" x 37½"

From the diagonally striped binding fabric, cut:
4 strips, 2½" x 42"

Two for the Work of One

The strips for this pattern were cut from the long side of a fat quarter. If you choose to use strips from a full-width cut of fabric (42" wide), you can make centers for two quilts, without much additional work. Make one quilt for you, one quilt for a friend, or make a stash of quilts you can give away to your favorite people.

Piecing

1. Arrange the 22"-long strips as shown and sew them together to make a strip set. Press seam allowances in one direction.

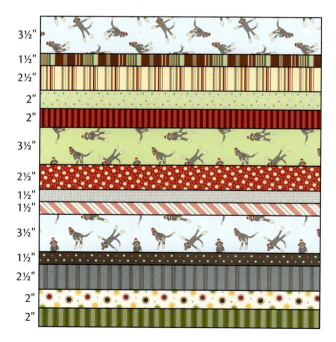

2. Using a rotary cutter and ruler, cut the strip set into three segments 7" wide.

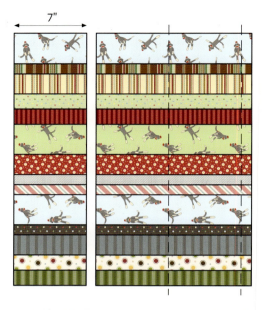

7"

3. Sew a 1¼" x 25½" brown strip to each side of a 1" x 25½" light green strip to create the vertical sashing. Press seam allowances toward the brown strips. Make two.

Make 2.

4. Lay out the quilt top, rotating the middle strip-set segment 180°. Place the two vertical sashing strips from step 3 between the strip-set segments. Sew the vertical units together and press the seam allowances toward the brown strips.

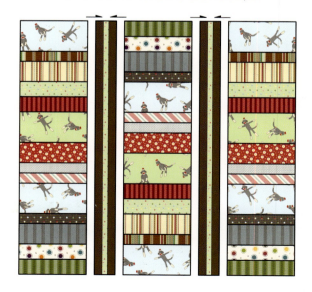

Adding the Borders

1. Sew 1½" x 25½" brown strips to each side of the quilt top. Press the seam allowances toward the brown strips. Sew the 1½" x 26" brown strips to the top and bottom; press.

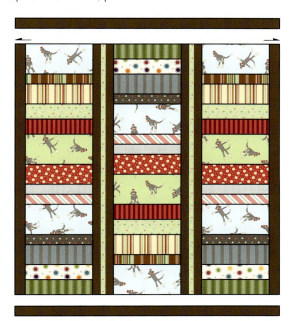

2. Sew the 5½" x 26" border strips to the top and bottom of the quilt. Press the seam allowances toward the border fabric. Sew 5½" x 37½" border strips to the sides; press.

Completing the Quilt

Refer to "Quilting and Finishing" beginning on page 19 for details as needed. A wavy grid of quilting fills the middle of the quilt. I quilted the borders with simple straight lines on either side of the small brown border and quilted the large outside border with small wavy lines along the diagonal stripes.

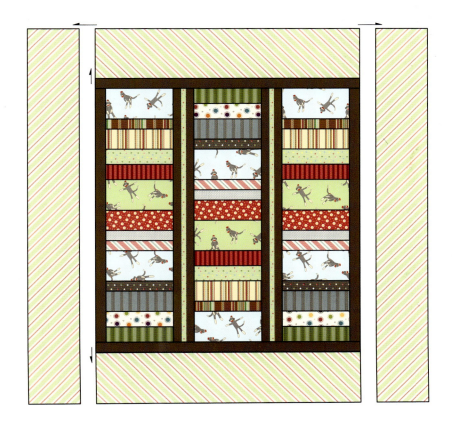

Finished Quilt: 41¼" x 41¼"
Finished Block: 9" x 9"

I took advantage of a marvelous Charm Pack to make this quick and easy quilt. The fruit and floral prints, bright stripes, and other prints remind me of a cheery kitchen. Whimsical raw-edge appliqué flowers give the quilt texture and visual interest. You can enjoy this quilt as a kitchen table topper while sipping your morning coffee or tea. Use soft juvenile prints, and you'll have a darling baby quilt to give warmth to a beloved infant or toddler.

Kitchen Basics

Materials

Yardage is based on 42"-wide fabric.

44 charm squares (5" x 5") for blocks
14 charm squares for appliqués (or use 5" x 5" or larger scraps)
1 charm square (5" x 5") for sashing squares
¾ yard of black fabric for outer border
⅓ yard of red-and-white polka-dot fabric for sashing
⅓ yard of red print for middle border
¼ yard of light green print for inner border
½ yard of diagonally striped fabric for binding
2⅞ yards of fabric for backing
45" x 45" piece of batting
Template material
Water-soluble fabric glue

Cutting

From the red-and-white polka-dot fabric, cut:
5 strips, 1½" x 42"; cut the strips into:
      2 strips, 1½" x 31½"
      8 rectangles, 1½" x 9½"
      2 rectangles, 1½" x 11½"

From the charm square for sashing squares, cut:
12 squares, 1¼" x 1¼"

From the light green print, cut:
4 strips, 1" x 42"

From the red print, cut:
4 strips, 2" x 42"

From the black fabric, cut:
4 strips, 5" x 42"

From the diagonally striped fabric, cut:
5 strips, 2½" x 42"

Cutting the Appliqués

Make templates for the appliqué pieces using the patterns on pages 51 and 52. Cut without adding a seam allowance for raw-edge appliqué.

From the assorted charm squares, cut:
2 *each* of templates A, B, C, D, and E (flowers)
8 of template F (leaves)
4 of template G (flower centers)
2 of template H (flower centers)
4 of template I (flower centers)

Piecing the Blocks

1. Sort the charm squares into the following groups. These groups will be sewn together into the blocks and setting blocks. Keep in mind that the quilt will look better when your groups are made up of different colors and prints to create contrast and interest.

   Group A: 5 groups of 4 charm squares for complete blocks

   Group B: 4 groups of 3 charm squares for side blocks

   Group C: 4 groups of 2 charm squares for corner blocks

   Group D: 2 groups of 2 charm squares for small appliquéd blocks

2. When making the Four Patch blocks, I suggest that you use chain piecing, described on page 14. Each block consists of two pairs of squares. When piecing, keep the two pairs next to each other in the line of chain piecing. Place the squares, right sides together, and sew a ¼" from the edge. Repeat with all pairs of squares. Clip threads between pairs, and press seam allowances in opposite directions for each pair, toward the darker fabric if possible.

 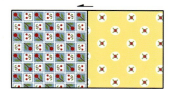

3. With right sides together, match the seams of each pair from step 2 and pin to secure. Repeat for all pairs, and sew the pinned blocks using

chain piecing. Clip the connecting threads and press seam allowances toward the darker fabrics.

Make 5.

4. The Group B charm squares are for the side setting blocks. Sew the first two squares together. Press the seam allowances toward the darker fabric. Make four.

5. Place the third square, right sides together on one of the sewn squares, aligning the raw edges. Sew perpendicular to the other seam and press seam allowances toward the darker fabric. Repeat to make four three-square units.

Make 4.

6. Sew the Group C charm squares together in pairs and press seam allowances toward the darker fabric. Make four.

7. The Group D charm squares will become the small Four Patch blocks that are added using the raw-edge appliqué technique. Mark the wrong side of one 5" square with three lines that are 1¼" apart and 1¼" from the raw edge. Repeat with one of the other squares.

1¼" 1¼" 1¼" 1¼"

8. Place the marked square and another 5" square right sides together and sew ¼" to the left of each marked line; then sew the right raw edge. Repeat the process with the other pair of squares.

9. Using a rotary cutter, cut on each marked line. Press seam allowances toward the darker fabric.

10. Align two strips, right sides together with opposite fabrics touching and seams butting together. Repeat steps 7, 8, and 9 to mark, sew, cut, and press. Repeat for all the strips to make eight small Four Patch blocks from each pair of squares, for a total of 16. Three will be extra.

Make 16.

Assembling the Quilt Center

1. Referring to "Raw-Edge Appliqué" on page 17, appliqué five small Four Patch blocks onto the larger Four Patch blocks, matching all four seams. Appliqué small Four Patch blocks onto all the side and corner setting blocks. *Don't do any trimming after you add the appliqué.*

2. Lay out the five Four Patch blocks on point with the sashing, side setting blocks, and the four corner setting blocks, as shown. Join the pieces in each diagonal row. Press seam allowances toward the setting pieces. Sew the rows together and press the seam allowances in one direction. Add the remaining corner setting blocks to the quilt center. Press the seam allowances toward the setting blocks.

3. Using the raw-edge appliqué technique, appliqué 12 sashing squares on top of the sashing, as shown.

4. Trim and square up the quilt top, leaving ¼" beyond the points of the side blocks. If all seam allowances are exact, the quilt should measure 28¾" x 28¾".

Adding the Borders

1. Referring to "Adding Borders" on page 14, measure, cut and sew the light green 1"-wide borders to the quilt. Press the seam allowances toward the border fabric.
2. Repeat to add the 2"-wide red border strips and the 5"-wide black border strips to the quilt. Press all seam allowances away from the quilt center.

Appliqué

Lay out the flowers, flower centers, and leaves on the quilt top in opposite corners using the illustration as a guide for placement, or place as desired. Pin or lightly glue each appliqué piece into place. Use the raw-edge appliqué method to appliqué each flower, flower center, and leaf to the quilt top.

Completing the Quilt

Refer to "Quilting and Finishing" beginning on page 19 for details as needed. I quilted each large Four Patch block with a flower and the small Four Patch blocks with a swirl for the flower centers. I quilted each sashing strip with a scroll pattern and each red sashing square appliqué with a swirl. I surrounded the red and green borders by straight stitching and quilted a scallop pattern in the black border.

C
Cut 2.

B
Cut 2.

A
Cut 2.

F
Cut 8.

G
Cut 4 for flowers A and D.

H
Cut 2 for flower B.

I
Cut 4 for
flowers C and E.

D
Cut 2.

E
Cut 2.

Finished Quilt: 61" x 72½"
Finished Block: 6" diamond

Create your very own sparkling diamonds with this simple technique. You'll have all you want once you learn how to make these strip-pieced beauties. You can use Jelly Rolls or cut your own strips. Either way, learning this technique will open up new possibilities for designing your own unique quilts.

Dripping Diamonds

Materials

Yardage is based on 42"-wide fabric.

1 Jelly Roll (40 strips, 2½" x 42")*
2 yards of brown floral for outer border
¾ yard of blue paisley print for setting triangles
¼ yard of red print for flat piping
⅝ yard of fabric for binding
4 yards of fabric for backing
67" x 79" piece of batting
*If cutting strips from your stash, you'll need 39 strips, 2½" x 42".

Cutting

From the blue paisley print, cut:
3 strips, 7½" x 42"

From the red print, cut:
7 strips, 1" x 42"

From the brown floral, cut on the *lengthwise* grain:
4 strips, 6½" x 65"

From the binding fabric, cut:
7 strips, 2½" x 42"

Piecing the Blocks

1. Organize your Jelly Roll strips into sets of three strips each. Two strips should be similar in value and the third strip a contrasting value.

2. Piece your strips of three so the middle strip is the contrasting value. Repeat to make 13 strip sets. Press strips well using a hot iron. Take care not to distort fabric when pressing. Divide the strip sets into two groups, one group of seven strip sets and one of six.

Prevent Stretching

Use spray starch when pressing the strip sets; this will help prevent stretching and distortion.

3. For the group of seven strip sets, line up the 60° line on the ruler with the top raw edge of the strip set. Accuracy is of the utmost importance. Cut the strip set along the ruler's edge to make a diagonal cut. Repeat until all seven strip sets are cut.

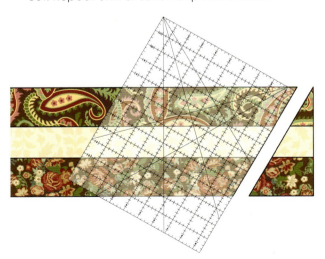

4. To cut the diamonds, rotate the strip set and line up the 6½" line on your ruler with the 60° angled cut; cut the diamond block, and continue to cut each diamond 6½" from the previous cut. I make two cuts, and then check to make sure the 60° angle is still accurate. Trim to fix the angle if necessary, and then continue cutting. You should be able to cut five diamonds from each strip set. Repeat until all strip sets are cut.

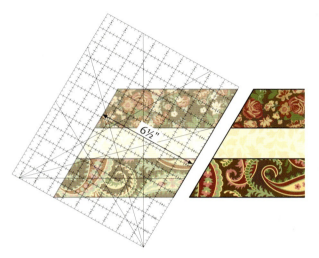

5. For the remaining six strip sets, use the same process as in step 3, but cut a 60° angle in the opposite direction. Cut all six strip sets. You will have several extra diamonds, but this will give you more flexibility and greater variety in your blocks.

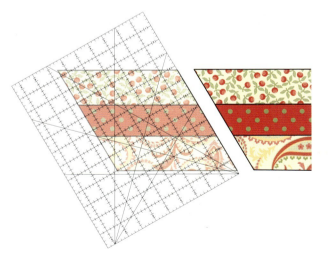

6. From the 7½"-wide blue paisley strips, make a 60° cut (the direction of the angle doesn't matter this time) on one end. Rotate the strip, line up the 7½"

line with 60° angled cut, and cut 7½" diamonds. You should be able to cut four per strip, for a total of 12. These setting diamonds are cut larger for ease in piecing.

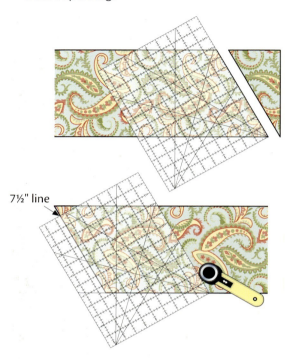

7½" line

7. Cut four of the diamonds from step 6 in half lengthwise (for the sides), and cut eight diamonds in half along the width (for the top, bottom, and corners).

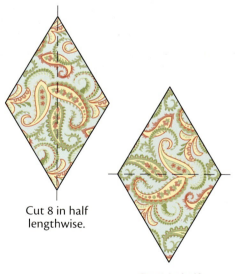

Cut 8 in half lengthwise.

Cut 8 in half widthwise.

Assembling the Quilt Top

1. Arrange the diamond blocks in diagonal rows as shown. Alternate the blocks cut from the seven strip-set group with diamonds cut from the six strip-set group. The rows will have alternating angles that make the blocks look like they are woven.

2. Add the setting pieces, placing the long diamonds on the sides and the equilateral triangles along the top, bottom, and corners.

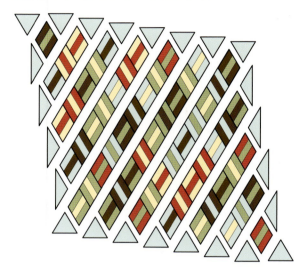

3. To piece the diamond blocks, place right sides together and line up raw edges. Align the blocks to make a "valley" ¼" from each edge being pieced. You can insert a pin at the point where the ¼" seam allowances meet to help you line up the blocks.

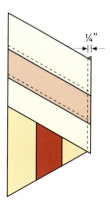

¼"

4. Piece the diamonds and setting pieces together into diagonal rows. Repeat until all the rows are pieced. Press the seam allowances in opposite direction from row to row. Join the diagonal rows and press seam allowances in one direction.

5. Trim the quilt top ½" beyond each diamond point. Make sure the corners are square.

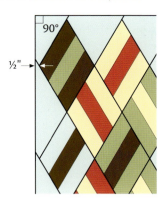

Adding the Flat Piping and Borders

1. Prepare the flat piping. For each quilt side, sew two 1"-wide red strips together on the diagonal. Press the seam allowances to one side. Fold the strips in half lengthwise wrong sides together, and press.

2. Cut one of the 1"-wide strips into two 21"-length strips. For the top piping, sew the 1" x 42" strip to the 1" x 21" strip, on the diagonal. Trim and press the seam allowances to one side. Fold the strip in half lengthwise wrong sides together and press. Make two.

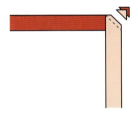

3. Using a scant ¼" seam allowance, sew the folded piping to the right side of the top and bottom of the quilt, ensuring that the raw edges are even with the raw edge of quilt. Repeat for the sides. Trim excess at the corners as needed.

4. Referring to "Adding Borders" on page 14, measure, cut, and sew the 6½"-wide outer-border strips to the quilt. Press the seam allowances toward the border fabric.

Completing the Quilt

Refer to "Quilting and Finishing" beginning on page 19 for details as needed. I quilted along the diagonal rows in a vine-and-scroll pattern. There is no quilting on the folded piping, and the border is quilted in a vine-and-scroll pattern as well.

Finished Quilt: 59¾" x 59¾"
Finished Block: 7⅝" x 7⅝"

Bright, fun colors and whimsical appliqué invite you to sit and dream awhile as you snuggle in this sweet and quirky quilt. Here's a chance to use Jelly Rolls for the quilt center and a gorgeous large-scale print in the borders.

Up a Tree

Materials

Yardage is based on 42"-wide fabric.

1 Jelly Roll (40 strips, 2½" x 42")
2 yards of brown large-scale print for outer border
½ yard of brown print 1 for tree
⅓ yard of pink striped fabric for inner border
10" x 14" piece of yellow wool for bird
2" x 20" piece of brown print 2 for branch
3" x 5" piece *each* of 3 different green wools for leaves
⅔ yard of plaid for bias binding
4 yards of fabric for backing
Embroidery floss to match wool
66" x 66" piece of batting
Template material

Cutting

The appliqué patterns are on page 62.

From the pink striped fabric, cut:
5 strips, 1½" x 42"; crosscut one of the strips into 4 pieces, 1½" x 10"

From brown large-scale print, cut on the *lengthwise* grain:
4 strips, 6½" x 62"

From the brown print 1, cut:
1 strip, 6" x 42"
1 strip, 6" x 12"

From the yellow wool, cut:
1 bird

From the green wool, cut:
3 leaves

From the plaid, cut:
2½"-wide bias strips to total 252"

Piecing the Blocks

1. Organize your Jelly Roll strips into color groups. These instructions refer to the colors used in the quilt shown, but substitute colors from your own Jelly Roll as appropriate. Group strips of like colors into sets of four strips each: three sets of four blues, two sets *each* of four pinks and four greens, one set *each* of four browns, four reds, and four yellows.

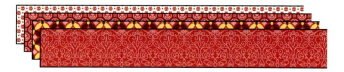

Examples of color groups:
4 reds and 4 greens

2. Sew each set of four strips together to make a strip set. Press the seam allowances all in the same direction. You will have 10 strip sets. Cut each strip set into 8½" squares; you should get four or five squares from each for a total of 40 to 50 squares.

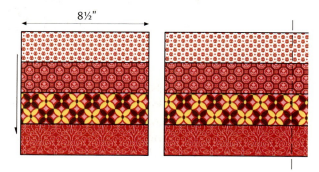

8½"

3. Pair up the squares as you would like them to appear in the blocks. I made the following color pairings in the quilt shown: five pairs of pink and blue, five pairs of blue and green, three pairs of pink and brown, three pairs of green and red, one pair of yellow and brown, one pair of yellow and red. You need 36 blocks, so there will be extra squares from the strip sets. Make extra blocks for variety and use the leftovers for another project or in the backing of your quilt.

4. Place the pairs right sides together and mark a diagonal line on the wrong side of one of the blocks. Pin the pairs together, with seams nesting. Sew ¼" on each side of the marked line. Using a rotary cutter, cut on the marked line. Press the seam allowances of each block toward the darker fabric. Repeat for all the pairs.

Assembling the Quilt Top

1. Lay out the blocks in six rows of six blocks, arranging them as shown.

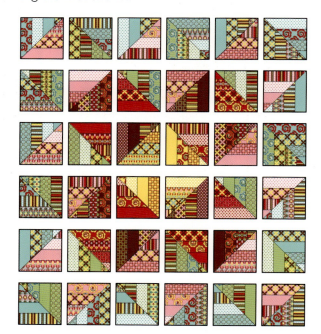

2. Join the blocks in each horizontal row. Press seam allowances to the right on odd-numbered rows, and press seam allowances to the left on even-numbered rows. Join the rows and press all seam allowances toward the bottom.

Appliqué

1. Remove the selvage ends from the 6"-wide brown print 1 strips and sew them together to make one long piece, approximately 6" x 53" for the tree trunk.
2. Referring to "Raw-Edge Appliqué" on page 17 and the appliqué placement diagram, appliqué the branch and trunk onto the quilt top. Trim to fit as desired.
3. Referring to "Wool Appliqué" on page 17, appliqué the wool bird and leaves onto the quilt top, placing them as shown, or as desired.

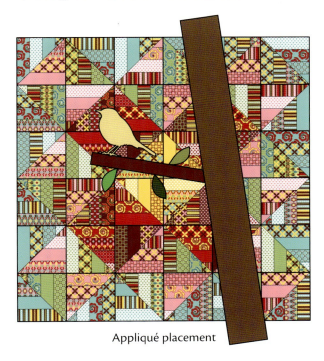

Appliqué placement

Adding the Borders

1. Sew a 1½" x 10" pink striped strip to each of the 1½" x 42" pink striped strips to make them long enough to fit the quilt. Press seam allowances to one side.
2. Referring to "Adding Borders" on page 14, sew the 1½"-wide border strips to the top and bottom of the quilt. Press seam allowances toward the border fabric. Add the side borders and press.
3. Repeat the process to add the 6½"-wide outer-border strips to the top and bottom of the quilt, and then add the sides. Press seam allowances toward the border fabric.

Completing the Quilt

Refer to "Quilting and Finishing" beginning on page 19 for details as needed. For the quilting, I used vines, swirls, and leaves in an allover pattern. I straight stitched each side of the inner border and quilted in the fabric pattern of the outer border.

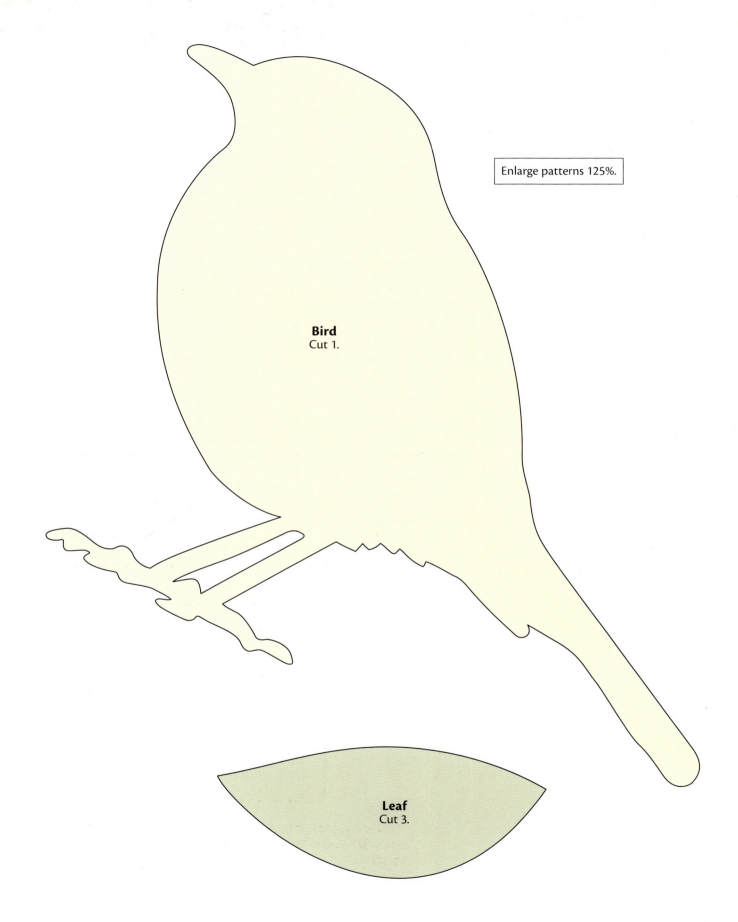

Enlarge patterns 125%.

Bird
Cut 1.

Leaf
Cut 3.

Finished Quilt: 52" x 58"

Here's a wonderful way to use your large-scale fabrics! You can put your favorites all together without having them clash. This is a delightful and quick quilt to make for a friend, for hanging on a wall, or simply for the pleasure of quilting.

Circle of Friends

Materials

Yardage is based on 42"-wide fabric.

1 yard of light striped fabric for circles background
½ yard of red-and-white floral for top border
½ yard of large-scale red-and-white print for left border
1 fat quarter of light print for upper-left corner
16 assorted squares, 10" x 10", for appliqué circles
½ yard of diagonally striped fabric for binding
3¼ yards of fabric for backing
3½ yards of jumbo green rickrack (1½" wide)
1¼ yards of 20"-wide lightweight interfacing
58" x 64" piece of batting
Template material
Water-soluble fabric glue

Cutting and Marking

There's a lot of room to play with this quilt; you don't have to be exact, which is fun for a change.

1. Using your rotary cutter, straighten each edge of the yard cut of fabric, both half-yard cuts of fabric, and the fat quarter.
2. Mark the one-yard background piece by folding it in half lengthwise three times. Press with an iron. Fold in half widthwise three times and press. Mark the intersections of the pressed lines as shown. This will indicate the position for the center of each appliquéd circle.

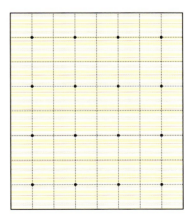

3. Make a full-circle template using the quarter-circle pattern on page 66, and trace the template onto each of the 10" squares.
4. From the binding fabric, cut six strips, 2½" x 42".

Preparing the Circles

1. Divide the 16 marked squares into two piles of 8. Half of your circles will be appliquéd with the raw-edge technique, and the other half will be appliquéd using the machine-appliqué method.
2. For the raw-edge appliquéd circles, cut the circles out along the drawn line. Find the center of each circle by folding in half twice and finger-pressing. Pin the center of the circle to every other creased intersection on the background.
3. Referring to "Machine Appliqué" on page 16, cut the remaining circles ½" outside the drawn line and prepare them using lightweight inter-facing. Find the center of each circle and pin it to the background on the remaining creased intersections.
4. Adhere each circle to the background using a water-soluble glue.

Appliqué

1. Refer to "Raw-Edge Appliqué" on page 17 and sew the raw-edge circles to the background fabric ¼" from the raw edges. You can choose a matching-color thread, clear monofilament thread, or white thread.
2. For the machine-appliqué circles, use the method described in "Machine Appliqué" on page 16. Use a like-color thread or a monofila-ment thread for the spool thread, and the bobbin thread should match the background fabric.

Adding Borders and Rickrack

1. With right sides together, sew the large-scale red-and-white left-border piece to the appliquéd background along the long edge. Press the seam allowances toward the border. Use a ruler and rotary cutter to straighten and square up the edges as needed.

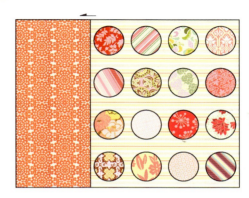

2. With right sides together, sew the light print upper-left corner piece to the red-and-white floral top-border piece, short sides together. Press seam allowances to the right. Using a ruler and rotary cutter, straighten the edges.

3. Join the units from steps 1 and 2 together, matching the seams. Press seam allowances toward the top border. Trim the top border to align with the bottom unit.

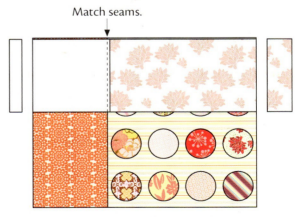

Sew and trim.

4. Center the rickrack along the horizontal seam line and trim it to the length needed. Pin and topstitch the rickrack into place using matching thread and a straight stitch.

5. Repeat step 4 to sew rickrack along the vertical seam line.

Completing the Quilt

Refer to "Quilting and Finishing" beginning on page 19 for details as needed. I quilted the circles in the quilt with off-center spirals and stipple quilted the background. The rest of the quilt was quilted using the fabric print as a guide. I quilted many flowers, leaves, and fun grid designs as the fabric determined.

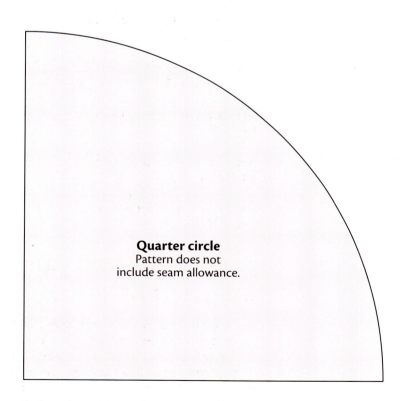

Quarter circle
Pattern does not
include seam allowance.

Finished Quilt: 53½" x 79"
Finished Block: 8½" x 8½"

Layer Cakes allow you to make this charming quilt for nearly instant gratification. Indulge in a fun stack of fabrics and revel in the ease of stacking, cutting, switching, and sewing. You'll love this simple method, and you'll enjoy your new quilt even more.

Griddle Cakes

Materials

Yardage is based on 42"-wide fabric.

1 Layer Cake or 40 assorted squares, 10" x 10"
½ yard of red striped fabric for pieced outer border
½ yard of brown floral for pieced outer border
⅜ yard of brown print for inner border
⅓ yard of green striped fabric for pieced outer border
¼ yard of off-white print for pieced outer border
⅝ yard of dark brown print for binding
4¾ yards of fabric for backing
60" x 85" piece of batting

Cutting

From the brown print, cut:
7 strips, 1½" x 42"

From the red striped fabric, cut:
1 strip, 12½" x 42"

From the brown floral, cut:
1 strip, 12½" x 42"

From the green striped fabric, cut:
1 strip, 9" x 42"

From the off-white print, cut:
1 strip, 5" x 42"

From the dark brown print, cut:
7 strips, 2½" x 42"

Organizing and Cutting the Squares

1. Organize your 10" squares into six stacks of six and one stack of four, right sides up. Stack your fabrics to include different colors, patterns, and scales in each stack. Layer large-scale prints next to small-scale ones, plaids next to florals, and so on. Each finished block will include four different fabrics.
2. Align the raw edges of the squares precisely in each stack. You'll cut each stack in the same manner, including the stack

of four fabrics. Cut through all six fabrics (or four) in one stack at the same time with your rotary cutter in the order given.

First: Cut 2" from the left edge.
Second: Cut 2½" from the first cut.
Third: Cut 2" from the top edge.
Fourth: Cut 1½" from the third cut.

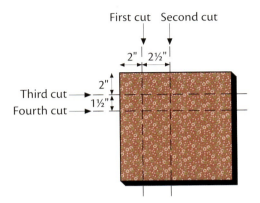

3. Working with one stack at a time, leave A, E, G, and I alone. Move the top layer of B and F to the bottom. Move the top two layers of pieces C and H to the bottom. Move the top three layers of piece D to the bottom. For the stack with only four layers, leave the D pieces as they are.

Piecing

The most effective way to sew the blocks together is by chain piecing (page 14). Chain piece only one set of pieces together at a time, to prevent confusion. Take care to keep the pieces in the correct order as you sew and press. I keep the units from one stack connected by thread until I'm done pressing.

1. Join pieces A and B from each layer; press seam allowances toward piece A. Clip the threads and place the units back in order.
2. Join pieces C and D; press seam allowances toward D. Clip the threads and place the units back in order.
3. Join pieces E and F; press seam allowances toward piece E. Clip threads and place the units back in order.
4. Join pieces G and H, press seam allowances toward H. Clip the threads and replace in order.
5. Join unit GH to I; press seam allowances toward I. Clip the threads and place back in order.
6. Join unit AB to CD; press seam allowances toward AB. Clip the threads and replace in order.
7. Join unit ABCD to EF; press seam allowances toward ABCD. Clip the threads and replace in order.
8. Join unit ABCDEF to GHI; press seam allowances toward GHI. Clip the threads and your blocks are complete!

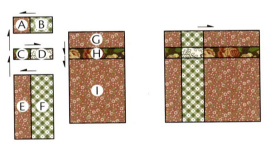

9. Repeat steps 1–8 with the remaining stacks to make a total of 40 blocks.

Assembling Quilt Center

1. Arrange the blocks in eight rows of five blocks each. Rotate the blocks as shown in the quilt diagram, or as you prefer.

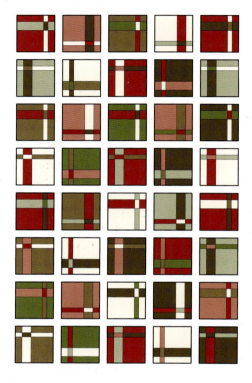

2. Join the blocks in each horizontal row. Press seam allowances to the right on odd-numbered rows, and press seam allowances to the left on even-numbered rows. Join the rows and press all seam allowances toward the bottom.

Adding the Borders

1. Sew two 2½" x 42" brown print strips together, end to end. Repeat to make two side borders. Press seam allowances in one direction. Piece three strips together for the top and bottom borders.
2. Referring to "Adding Borders" on page 14, measure the length of the quilt through the center; cut and add the side borders. Press seam allowances toward the brown print. Measure the width through the center; cut and add the top and bottom borders. Press.
3. Sew the 12½"-wide red striped, 9"-wide green striped, 5"-wide off-white, and 12½"-wide brown floral border strips together as shown to make a strip set. Press seam allowances all in the same

direction. From this strip set, cut eight segments, 5" wide.

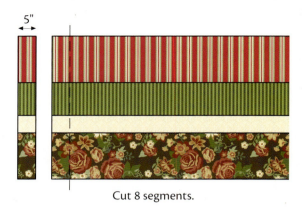

Cut 8 segments.

4. Join the strip-set segments from step 3 end to end in pairs to make four border strips.

Make 4.

5. Measure the quilt as you did before and trim the side borders to the length needed. Sew them to the quilt top. Press seam allowances toward the outer borders. Repeat to add the top and bottom borders.

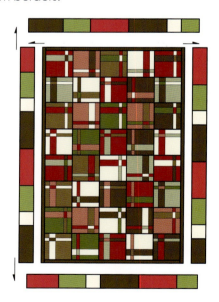

Completing the Quilt

Refer to "Quilting and Finishing" beginning on page 19 for details as needed. I quilted the squares with alternating big and small cinnamon-bun swirls. I quilted two straight lines on either side of the inner border. I quilted the outer border in a pattern of vines and swirls.

Finished Quilt: 31½" x 31½"

Using precut charm squares results in a quilt that comes together quickly and with such amazing results. It's so simple and speedy, you'll want to keep making more—as gifts, baby blankets, table toppers, or wall art.

Charming Garden

Materials

Yardage is based on 42"-wide fabric.

25 assorted light- to medium-value charm squares, 5" x 5", for quilt center*
24 assorted medium- to dark-value charm squares, 5" x 5", for border**
Assorted scraps for appliqués:
    1 piece, 2" x 8" *each of 3 different* green fabrics for stems
    1 piece, 3" x 4" *each of 3 different* green fabrics for leaves
    1 square, 7" x 7" of red fabric for flower
    1 square, 5" x 5" of blue fabric for flower
    1 square, 5" x 5" of white fabric for flower
    1 square, 3" x 3" of brown fabric for flower
    1 square, 3" x 3", of red fabric for flower
⅜ yard of diagonally striped fabric for binding
1 yard of fabric for backing
36" x 36" piece of batting
3 yards of green rickrack (1" wide)
Template material
Water-soluble fabric glue (optional)
*Or ⅔ yard total of light- to medium-value scraps
**Or ½ yard total of medium- to dark-value scraps

Cutting

If you bought Charm Packs, happy day—you don't have to cut a thing! If you're using fabric from your stash, enjoy selecting fabrics and cut the following squares.

From the assorted light- to medium-value fabrics, cut:
25 squares, 5" x 5"

From the assorted medium- to dark-value fabrics, cut:
24 squares, 5" x 5"

From the diagonally striped fabric, cut:
4 strips, 2½" x 42"

Assembling the Quilt Top

1. Use the 25 lightest-value squares for the center of the quilt. Arrange the squares randomly in five rows of five squares each. Try to keep like colors from being next to each other.

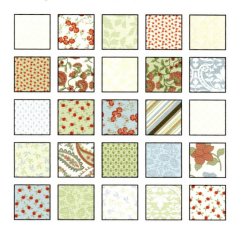

2. Sew the squares together in rows. Press the seam allowances to one side, alternating the direction of the seam allowances from one row to the next. Sew rows together. Press the seam allowances toward the bottom of the quilt.

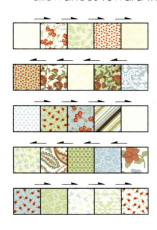

3. Cut the rickrack into four 23" lengths and align one piece with each raw edge of the quilt. The outer edge of the zigzag points should touch the raw edge of the quilt. Using a longer stitch length, machine baste the rickrack to the quilt top using a scant ¼" seam allowance.

4. Lay the quilt top face up and arrange the remaining darker squares around it to create the border. Try to keep like colors from being next to each other. Join the side-border squares together. Press the seam allowances toward the top of the quilt. Join the side borders to the quilt top. Press the seam allowances toward the borders.

5. Join the squares to make the top and bottom borders. Press the seam allowances to the left. Join the top and bottom borders to the quilt top. Press the seam allowances toward the borders.

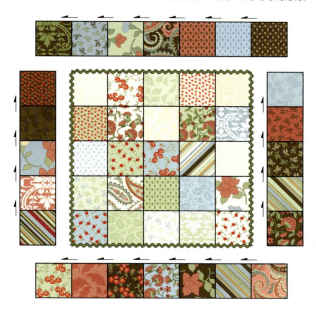

Appliqué

The patterns for the flower and leaf appliqués are on pages 74 and 75. Refer to "Raw-Edge Appliqué" on page 17 as needed for detailed instructions.

1. Make templates for the flowers, flower centers, stems, and leaves. Trace the shapes onto the fabrics and cut them out on the drawn lines.

2. Place the appliqués on the quilt in the desired location or refer to the photograph on page 72 for guidance. Pin or glue the leaves and stems.

3. Appliqué the leaves and stems. Then appliqué the flowers, followed by the flower centers.

Completing the Quilt

Refer to "Quilting and Finishing" beginning on page 19 for details as needed. I quilted leaves, scrolls, and flowers in an allover pattern. I quilted the appliqués following the flowers, stems, and leaves.

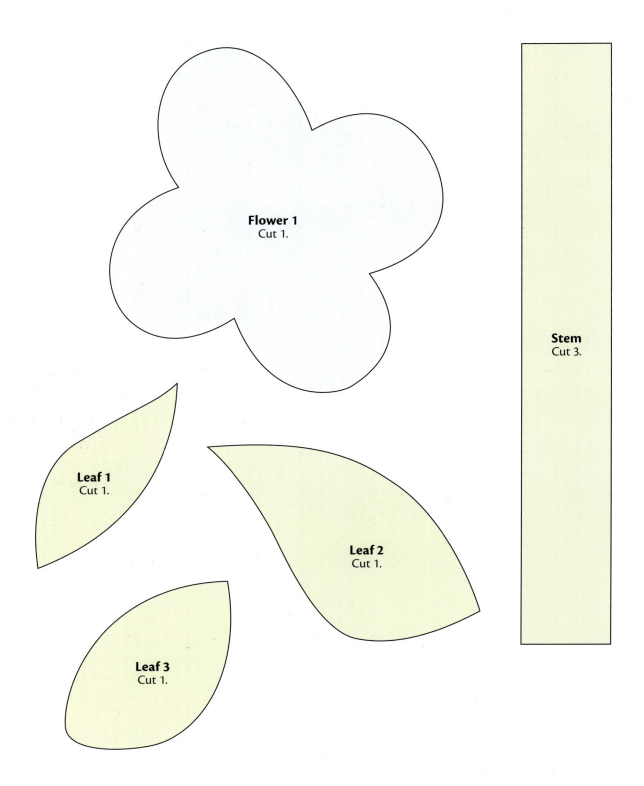

Flower 1
Cut 1.

Stem
Cut 3.

Leaf 1
Cut 1.

Leaf 2
Cut 1.

Leaf 3
Cut 1.

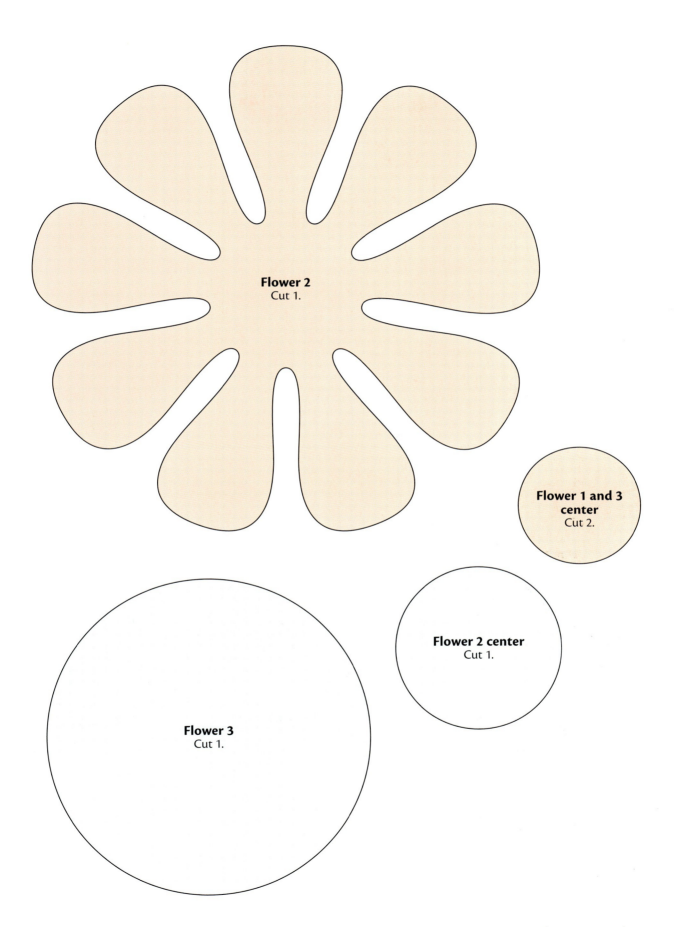

Flower 2
Cut 1.

Flower 1 and 3 center
Cut 2.

Flower 2 center
Cut 1.

Flower 3
Cut 1.

Finished Quilt: 40" x 40½"
Finished Blocks: 8" x 8" and 3¾" x 3¾"

This simple but striking quilt uses precut charm squares and a couple of favorite fabrics. Made in soft colors, it's ideal for a beloved baby. Use bold or subtle colors if you're choosing to make a quilt for an empty wall calling for some art. Whatever colors you choose, you'll make this quilt in no time at all and have a blast doing it.

Wheelin' It

Materials

Yardage is based on 42"-wide fabric.

23 assorted light-value charm squares, 5" x 5"
23 assorted medium- to dark-value charm squares, 5" x 5"
⅔ yard of light print for borders
⅜ yard of brown print 1 for borders
⅛ yard of brown print 2 for flat piping
½ yard of dark brown print for binding
2⅝ yards of fabric for backing
46" x 47" piece of batting
10" x 10" piece of lightweight interfacing

Cutting

From the light print, cut:
4 strips, 4½" x 42"
2 strips, 1" x 42"

From brown print 1, cut:
2 strips, 3" x 42"
2 strips, 1¾" x 42"

From brown print 2, cut:
2 strips, 1" x 42"

From the dark brown print, cut:
5 strips, 2½" x 42"

Piecing the Blocks

1. Organize the charm squares into groups of four. Each group should contain two squares of like colors in a light value and two squares of like color in a darker value. Make 11 stacks of four charm squares each. You'll have one light and one dark charm square left over. Set these aside.

Make 11 stacks of 4 squares.

Working with Charm Packs

When using a purchased package of precut charm squares, you may have to be creative in your pairings. The most important rule is to have two darker values and two lighter values. If you're unsure if the pairing looks right, view it from a distance, and the values will become obvious.

2. Place a light- and dark-value square right sides together. Draw a diagonal line from corner to corner on the wrong side of the lighter square. Repeat for all squares.

3. Using chain piecing (page 14), sew the pairs of squares ¼" from both sides of the diagonal line. Cut each square on the marked diagonal line. Press seam allowances toward the darker fabric. Repeat for all the remaining pairs of squares.

4. Make the large Pinwheel block by sewing four half-square-triangle units together as shown. Sew the top two units together and press the seam allowances to the right. Sew the bottom two units together and press the seam allowances to the left. Butt the seams together and pin the top row to the bottom row. Sew and press. Make 11 large Pinwheel blocks. Trim the blocks to 8½" x 8½", ensuring you have the 4¼" point of your ruler on the center of the block. Note that I mixed and matched several of the half-square-triangle units to make scrappier blocks.

5. To make the small Pinwheel blocks place the two remaining charm squares right sides together. Using a pencil, draw two diagonal lines, making an X on the wrong side of the lighter square. Sew ¼" away on each side of each diagonal line.

6. Using a rotary cutter, cut on the marked diagonal lines. Without moving the pieces, cut the block in half horizontally and vertically. This will make eight small half-square-triangle units. Press the seam allowances toward the darker fabric. Repeat step 4 to make the two smaller Pinwheel blocks; do not trim the blocks. They should measure 3¾" x 3¾".

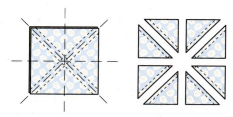

Assembling the Quilt Center

Arrange the large Pinwheel blocks in two rows of five blocks each. Sew the blocks into rows. Press the seam allowances of the top row to the left and press the seam allowances of the bottom row to the right. Sew the two rows together; press.

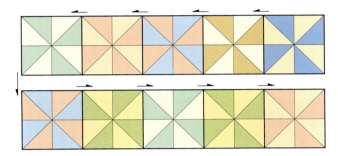

Adding Flat Piping and Borders

1. Fold the 1"-wide brown print strips in half length-wise, and press with a hot iron. Trim each strip to 40½" long.
2. Using a scant ¼" seam allowance, sew the flat piping to the top and bottom of the Pinwheel center with raw edges aligned.

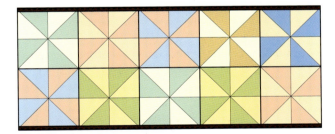

3. Prepare the top and bottom borders by sewing the strips together as shown. Press seam allowances toward the dark fabric. Trim the border units to 40½" long.

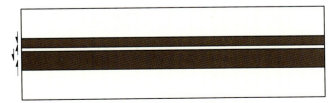

Make 2.

4. Using a ¼" seam allowance, add the top and bottom borders. Be sure to place the borders so that the wider brown border is closest to the quilt center.

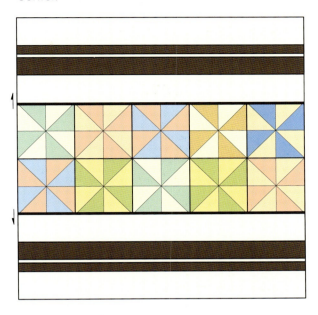

Appliqué

1. Referring to "Machine Appliqué" on page 16, prepare the 8½" Pinwheel block for appliqué using interfacing.
2. Pin the larger Pinwheel block and the two small Pinwheel blocks in place, centered over the darker strips, referring to the quilt photo on page 76 for placement guidance. Machine appliqué the large Pinwheel in place.
3. Refer to "Raw-Edge Appliqué" on page 17 and stitch the small Pinwheels in place.

Completing the Quilt

Refer to "Quilting and Finishing" beginning on page 19 for details as needed. I quilted the Pinwheel blocks with varying sizes of swirls and used a wave pattern in the borders. Be careful not to quilt on top of the folded piping.

About the Author

Sarah Bisel was born and raised in Salt Lake City, Utah. She attended Brigham Young University, where she received a B.S. in Finance. Sarah currently resides in sunny Arizona with her four beautiful children and the most wonderful man in the world.

Sarah enjoys her hectic lifestyle. After a long day of doing dishes, laundry, housecleaning, giving hugs, wiping hands, and helping with homework, she finds joy spending time in her fabulous sewing room, handling fabric, designing new patterns, and teaching her children (and sometimes hubby) about her love of quilting.

Sarah began her first quilt at the age of 18, hoping she could express herself through fabric. She quickly fell in love with the art of quilting. Years later, after embarking on the joys of motherhood, she began quilting again. She immersed herself in every quilting and design book she could get her hands on. Through the years, she found there was more than art in each quilt she made; there was also a little piece of her heart. She now wants to share her love of quilting with others and hopes as new quilters are born, more little pieces of her heart will be spread to friends, family, and neighbors around the world.

There's More Online!

To read Sarah's blog, visit www.milkandhoneydesigns.blogspot.com. To find more great books on quilting, knitting, crochet, and more, visit www.martingale-pub.com.